POETS UNDER GROUND VOLUME ONE

Poets Underground Press LLC
Poetsundergroundpress.com

Publication by Poets Underground Press LLC on January 17th, 2023

ISBN: 979-8-218-12286-7

FOREWORD

This is an Anthology made for the people
All people
Created by a group of poets apart of the Poets Underground movement that was born in
San Diego, California in 2019.
The Anthology highlights the best of 46 Poets sampled individual collections and is separated alphabetically for your easy participation.
With all the love and luck in the world, this book has found itself to your hands to read.
Enter now into the vault of our worlds and connect with us to connect back to you.

Welcome

to the Underground...

46

POET

Alexis Goodfellow

Alexis Goodfellow is a software engineer, jazz musician, puppeteer, chess hustler, & performance poet. She is a former Poets Underground headliner & was a San Diego native, but now based out of New Orleans & working on her second poetry collection. You can order her first collection ("Love Songs in the Key of Sorrow") wherever you can find books sold online.

Throwaway Sonnet

This is another piece to throw away
To line the wastebin's drooling eager lip
Where all the crumpled wide-ruled corpses stay
Reflections of an author's failing grip
The characters upon the torn up ream?
Underdeveloped and dimensionless
With structure, metaphor, and rhyming scheme
Quite overdone, cliché, and trite at best
But in the white page sea there must be fish
(Perhaps a mighty whale there might exist!)
Concealed in oceanic squid ink spray
So, with the open jaws of vicious shark
Exsanguinate these symbols of my heart—
Until, again, this "sonnet's" thrown away

For My Unicorn

You heard me scream my loneliness
Like the prideful lion's longing wail
Atop Saharan rock
Lacking fuel for the chase
You, the ibex who ran to me
Willingly embedding your neck
In my slack-jawed maw—
I believed you a mirage
Yet soon you left
Trotting on the horizon
Enough flavor on my tongue
To soldier on to sunrise
I followed your illusory haze
In blistering heat through baking air
Paws holding firm in loosened sand
While parched and starved
You brought me to oasis
Where I bathed with you
Disappearing into stillness
The only waves our footsteps
With wonder I beheld you
Resplendent in your grace
Flowing free in the water
Sparkling and bubbling

Having drunk from your trough
The waters receded
Your visage again filtered
By scalding Saharan haze
And there you wept
Preened white coat relinquished
For thick practical fur
To wither the weather
And there I wept
Hoping the tears
Would refract your striking light
Forming two horns back to one

Your eye-born pearls and mine
Both lost in the stack of grain
I held you again by the neck
And raised you to stand
Then set off again
To cross the ocean of sand
Questing for water
To feed my body and your beauty

Cutting through the dune
We'll walk together for some time—
And there along the path
Leave our weathered fur behind

The Loner's Lament

I set out a banquet
In the warmth of my house
Said "be there by seven"
To each friend thereabout
I sat and I waited
As the clock crept with cane
Then nobody, nobody
Nobody came
"Come with me to see this!"
I'd say with a grin
"The show sounds amazing!"
She'd muse over gin
Then twenty times over
My wide smile would wane
When nobody, nobody,
Nobody came
I invited the town
When I first graced the stage
"Solo act for an hour"
Read the newspaper page
The first one of many
I had hoped to proclaim
But nobody, nobody
Nobody came
I asked all the neighbors
Trudging from door to door
Some said "yes" and then flaked

Like paint chips on the floor
No matter the method
The result was the same
And nobody, nobody,
Nobody came
To shower the baby
Be they boy, they, or girl—
To sleep in my spire
Gazing over the world—

To regard a white veil
My pale face in its frame—
No, nobody, nobody,
Nobody came

Now, I know you are busy
Drowning in your own way
While I drown my sorrows
In Mike's Hard Lemonade
I understand, truly
And absolve you of blame
Yet nobody, nobody,
Nobody came
I know well what I craft's
Not beloved by all
In Creator's grand scheme
My creations are small
I know your attendance
Would require a plane
Still nobody, nobody,

Nobody came
I don't expect grandeur
Nor an opulent place
No jewelry to rattle
From my wrists nor my face
I long not for money
Not for worldwide fame—
Just nobody, nobody,
Nobody came
When you wish you were there
I am sure you speak truth
Giving tidings of luck,
Of legs broken and bruised
I believe you, I do
But my feelings are plain
For nobody, nobody,
Nobody came
I know my fate someday
When my heart at last caves

What I'll see from above
As I go to the grave
Just a lonely stone slab
Carved with my chosen name
Where nobody, nobody
Nobody came

But still, I shall be there
At your special events

And still, I shall be there
With my sense and my cents
And still, I shall be there
To shield you from that pain—
Knowing somebody,
Somebody,
Somebody came

POET

Alyssa Grass

Healer, Poet, Artist, Lover

And I Wandered Under the Moon

Under the Sun
upon the ground
Left to write the clouds, the stars
my only friends, the birds
And the wind adopted me,
the most welcoming family is ever met.
Oh, the coziest of homes under the shade of the trees
And stones, precious treasures everywhere
And how many times this dirt caught my tears, soaking up my blood
How lucky
To be so abandoned
To feel it for so many years
until the spirits give to me with new eyes
clear vision
To see that my true love, can be felt
Universally.

POET

Andy Palasciano

Andy Palasciano has been in The San Diego Poetry Annual, The Penwood Review, The Knot Literary Review, and is proud to have been selected to be part of the Underground! His book is *The Warrior: The Tales of a Substitute Teacher and Job Coach* (Lymer & Hart), which is available on Amazon.

Porcupine

The Soul is not an energy,
But a master thereof

In goes the porcupine,
And out comes the dove

While owing all to its
Creator above

The Soul is not an energy,
But a producer-
Of love

Bat Meat

The trees this twilight was flooded with moth-like
birds that moved like bats. The fluttering betwixt the
Moss hives high in the amber was enough to drive you to
Tears. Why do the trees stand still?

Pasty

As a child,
I was dropped on my head
so many times, that I was called
"the bruised one."
I fell out of
cars,
off shoulders to ice,
and every time it brought me
closer to the meadow,
where the dogs were barking
and the flowers were tasty
like grass churning through
the blades
and with my head all pasty

POET

Angela Murrell

Inspired by Poets Underground in 2019, Angela broke her 10yr long hiatus from writing poems, performing at open mics & writing all new pieces. Covering topics like small business relief funding, doom scrolling, and [bad] habit forming in the 2020 P.U anthology, she is committed to evolving her style via new creations.

Woven

There was something about being young and idealistic, and raging with hormones.
Every line I wrote then was woven together with an angst for everything to be some better way,
and critical of it when it wasn't.

But as I've aged, have I become more tolerant - or is it that I'm more accepting of the patience it
takes for things to change. I seem to cope with the idea they might not ever change in my own
lifetime.

Why do the words that come to me now seem to rhyme less? Like a bit of magic has been lost
as a transition between my thoughts.

Of course, I'm still enraged, but it comes from being defeated rather than my body changing too
rapidly.

The trouble with my criticisms of this society, is that I have to face my role in it. When I was a
teenager, I didn't have this same idea of accountability. It was everyone else's fault.

Perhaps now I don't fuss about the acoustics of my words. They may not sound great together.
Perhaps I don't want my words to sound at all.

It's about time I lower my own boisterous voice, in an effort to hear others more clearly.

A new magic is unfolding – There's been a silence long enough to hear the whispers grow to
audible voices. Let their words weave a new tapestry so that my enragement can now come
from listening.

Transcript

What's there to say
That could be of comfort
Or helpful in anyway
Is there something?

Long term investment in humanity?
But how can that matter when
The short term is bleak for so many

Presented words are different
In print, it's your voice reading my words
But now I'm speaking
And i want it to be what I'd say
I hear, you have to pause
And you can make it an auditory experience.

Can you make a poem by
Just writing the transcript of your mind?

So many things are being said
Sometimes in pictures
I wish I could tell it as fast as I can dream it
Why would the things in my head
Be any better if said
And why mine over yours

Do you ever think of really great material
And never write it down
And then when you've got time
You're fresh out. Zilch.
The trick is to ramble until
The mind is convinced it has free reign
To say what's been holding in.

Aren't all our minds
Just going and going

Because we have to keep going
Even though there's so much existential dread and collective doom?
How do you lighten the mood
Read the room?
Feel safe?
Say something helpful?

And even to complain
Seems like a guilty endeavor
Shouldn't I be grateful (oh I am!)
I can't help but think
If this is my feeling...
How are so many people, specifically those directly impacted,
directly triggered - fucking living?

And don't we want just that. To live. We all just want to live?
Just live? With health, somewhere safe?
Somewhere to be ourselves? To have access to food, clean water,
shelter, education,
healthcare?

How do we disagree on that?

I'm not the only one staring at maps,
Wondering where to live? Or at what point did our ancestors make
the brave decision to move?

My paternal great grandfathers left Russia and Italy after WWI. I so
wish to know their
motivations.

Grief of our elderly isn't just about what moments of ours they have
missed. I grieve the lost
history, perspective, and advice my grandmother would be able to
give.

I don't want to move.

I want to live at home, my home where I am familiar and feel
psychologically safe. I don't want

to move?! I don't want anyone to have to move.

These thoughts must come to a break now
But I know that many of us are compartmentalizing.

Seemingly working, doing chores, caregiving, trying to self-care - all having little transcripts
stuck inside.

Please share yours with your people.
Even if they make no sense, ramble, trail off, etc. You've nothing to hide.
You're just trying to live.

Select-All, Undo

I'm **A** - but not as you might say

And no, not in a normal way.

I forget **y**, but I'm not close to **b**
I'm to the left, and a little above, **c**,
Learning to appreciate the new proximity.

Pressed for time, or one time
Singular, or combined
I might write, I might act -
Probably mechanical,
Definitely with tact -
Shifting on either side,
hoping to capitalize,
At least to start.

It's an **A**rt.

I don't really behave the same,
within the bounds of my frame
But with some control
I'm quite selective –

I worry when I'm in this state,
That for now, it's too late.
Since all attention is focused,
Lit up like summer locusts,
highlighting from start to end
What mistake will this mend?
With one purposeful push back
I've created no mark, just redact.

I used to be afraid of **z**
But now I'm above that
I always thought it of one use -
the undoing of the obtuse.

But it all changed,
When we got rearranged.
At opposite ends, me and **z**
Well, usually...
(But in this case, that's me and **L**)
So **z** and I, who used to bicker and yell,
Now share this great need to talk...
We shifted so easily,
Well, we thought it was caps lock.

What I couldn't put my finger on,
being at odds so long
Is that we failed to see our commons, (busy relishing in ad homonyms)
- but when our ends lost control,
It was so apparent, their vitriol
- that we didn't really know each other
And the words we could make together.

POET

Anthony Azzarito

COO of Poets Underground Press LLC, Father of Five, Partner for life to Sunny Rey, Publisher, Hip Hop/Rap Artist, Believer, Poet, U.S. Army Veteran

An Ode to Poets Underground

The beginning
All poets do awaken
for the call to be heard,
no longer forsaken.
Beneath the trees lives thy truest breath
To be hushed
and silenced never met.
At the intersection of urge and stillness comes
courage to release a substance out into the atmosphere, foreign yet non-toxic to temperament
To any human being,
an antidote
Into the stillness of the night
When the pen pierced paper pleasures
litter the floor,
before a stage is occupied
before a microphone acts as a host to the words that are needed to be set out into that dark night sky.
Purpose within pentameters
The purpose has a predetermined destination
the heart,
and then
a poet is born.

Fresh Pork

There is a love that exists at the
bottom of the well
the rarest type of love
Down in Marianas Trench of the soul
it exists there anxiously active.
If it's touched
burns the skin
plagues the mind
but for the best.

To show proof of this form of love
one could say it's best described by
grabbing your ribs and pulling them apart and revealing your heart
for all to see
to see the bloody beating bitch
A humans life source.
I found that love
And that well was dark and cold
Small drops of water, puddles were present
But it was real
Raw dirt diamond in the cut.

She sat in a way that would drive any man up the walls
thighs crossed,
one leg over the other
sun kissed skin exposed
dangling a willowy foot, toes pointed down
Biting that bottom lip
peering over at me as my eyes roll to the back of my head.
That is my love.
She winks at me as if the closing of her eyelids sealed that fragment
in time and it was capturing our connection
she stole it from the sandman
to keep for when we dream.

I
found
what
I was looking for
Or maybe it found me.
Sometimes that well is so deep that as you lower the bucket down, it never hits the bottom
it's never able to scoop up the water
The well is too dry
sometimes you dig down deep
and those fragile rough hands bring up nothing but dirt to damper the doubt even more so than before.
Keep those hands on that rope, boy
Lower away
over and over and over again
Love can surprise you
And what a sweet surprise she has been

Now my well
is overflowing

The Divide

We can feel it everywhere
It's in the food that we eat
The air we breath
In the sheets that we sleep

You can feel it
Division
Not multiplication

Subtracting every ounce of human dignity
Never thinking to add
To the equation

We are so quick to take away
Slow to give
And taught generationally never to give back

But who could blame us
Each habitual curse before its own
Kept the ball rolling
Spinning out of control

Down
Down
Down every slope

A steam roller going downhill
Smoothing the pavement
Designing the concrete to catch your cheek

You can feel it
When you brush past shoulder
Shrugged or unshrugged
At every shopping mall full of goods, we together can't afford

Social media platforms
Stacking the bar so high

Dancing like a 5G tree out of reach
Even the influencers can't keep
being rats in the race

This is when love breaks through
This is when you read the headlines about what they said would be bullshit good news
In a foreign utopia of unity
that's where redemption ravaged onto

You can feel it
There
It's been there all along
Pressed between the prisoner and his cell

As the pages are being torn out
We want our piece of the ink to rewrite all that they didn't let us speak

Where next time

We
Write
In
Blood

Where now THEY can really feel it

POET

April Bernadette San Roman

April is a mental health professional by day and novice writer by night. She is a nature enthusiast, avid reader and advocate for self-love. Through poetry she has found a space to explore her own healing. She is looking forward to how this creative outlet will guide her through life's journey.

Love Is Easy

He said
Loving you is the easy part
He said
I'm afraid I can't give you all those things

I said
It's okay to be afraid
I said
Don't let fear hold you back and regret it

He failed once more
He didn't ask for forgiveness
He just walked out the front door

I sat and I thought to myself
Why?

Days will go by
And I realize I missed fear by another name
Shame

A poison I do not have the antidote for
His pain a burden that brings him silence and solace all the same

For what he was looking for in women lies underneath his pain

Had he turned his heart inward
He would have remedied the strain
To give and receive love without any blame

And now as I sit, and I stare at that door frame
It's like looking in a mirror
Because in it, I could see my need to do the same

Shadow Work

A poem is a perfect place to blame someone else for your misery
Fortunately for me I'm into that sort of thing
I love being the victim it makes me perfectly relatable

Lucky for us
Our parents didn't have a clue about mental health and trauma
And had not found anyone to blame for not knowing their love
language

So instead, they gave us a generation of women who desperately
seek words of affirmation
And men who are convinced that their lack of love will be solved
with a woman's physical
affection

The shadow lurks at the surface
Keeping my inner child wounded
Or so that's what Tik Tok would have me believe

Because I need healing
And who is going to do that for me?
Recession in full swing
I work a side hustle and 40 hours a week
Therapy session…. How's 2023?
Oh and insurance please
Covid has me quarantined and no trip to Tulum could save me
Woe is me

Doubting my choices and everything that challenges me
Imposter syndrome…who doesn't get it?

I'm tired of fighting back against the systems of oppression designed
to hold me hostage
A Stockholm Syndrome of sorts is boiling up inside of me

I'm ready for a man to propose and take care of me

How anti-feminist of me that as a woman I want to be worshiped endlessly

If you can't beat 'em, join 'em
It may be easier to surrender to the victimhood

Poor me
Because I'm awakening to the bullshit and there's no tools for me to work it out
At least not in my lifetime
Where I can be free from the prison in my mind
I'm helpless like a tree

Codependency…. Someone chain themselves to me
Don't let them uproot me
If I don't grow through what I go through
I lose my creative edge that brings me the external validation I need

To temporarily escape my victim mentality
And trick my higher self into thinking that I've transcended my ego
The cockroach of the human entity
Indestructible
The infestation and destruction living inside of me
I'll act like I have humility
But the truth is
I'm a narcissist just like the rest of us
Seeking the weakness of others to prop myself up
Thank goodness for the saving grace of those less fortunate
Or I might not make it through each and every day
Because this shadow is a little more insidious
Suffice it to say

Tongue Tied

I'd more quickly shove my tongue down your throat
So we could get tongue tied together
Rather than hear you utter the words
"I love you"
With such dis-ease
Like Covid or Tuberculosis
Maybe it's allergies
An aversion to me and my love
That says won't you please let me worship you on my knees
Where do I want to eat?
Wherever
Because I needed you like food
Like air in my lungs
That's not love that's co-dependency
I see now that what we were chasing was
Tight lips and loose hips
To soothe feelings of neglect from our parents
Who did not know how to keep the peace
And found a way to use our innocence as weaponry
Six years old was the first time I ever tasted betrayal
But what did I know at the time
Other than the bitter taste it left with me
An acquired taste that I gladly accustomed myself to
I wish I was joking
But it's a twisted game I started playing
Subconsciously
To keep myself from total self-loathing
I want to deliver myself from evil
Because I am deserving of love, time and commitment
Rather I wrap myself up in pity
And hope that some guy will save me
He'll take my hand
And hold it ever so gently
To remind me that I'm pretty

I am searching for a love of reciprocity
That would quickly satiate me

And remind me that I am abundantly deserving of a love that is carefree
And speaks so articulately
There will be no reason to get tongue tied
Because when that love speaks
It's not silencing me
Rather I am so enthralled
That I can't help but just want to listen attentively

POET

Ashley Aleem

Azad (Ashley Aleem) flawed human. wounded healer. deep feeler. critical thinker. sensitive by nature. skeptic by nurture. psychotherapist by trade. writer. dancer. speaker. teacher. life-long learner. mental health advocate. cynical humanist. aspiring authentic. walking dialectic. daughter of Jila and Iraj. granddaughter of Valeh. Ashley/ Shaghayegh/Azad. humbled and grateful to be invited to be free as herself in actuality among a creative community.

#1

Mom always gets upset
When I use the word hate
Don't say that she says
That's a very strong word
You don't hate. That's ugly.
You look ugly when you're angry.
You're too pretty not to be happy.
Too lucky to be sad. Why so sarcastic?
Don't be sassy. Don't be brash.
Yeah, I have very strong feelings.
And yeah, I do sometimes hate
I'm aware though not everyone can truly relate
She doesn't understand
I've felt it down to my bones
From before even I understood it
Long before I was grown

When I say it, it's because it's the quickest way
To cut to the chase
And easily express
The intensity of anger and pain,
Disgust, resentment, disdain
That I feel so deeply, literally, physically

Emotions are called feelings
Because you know it in your body
All too well
The sensations are part of the bigger picture
The pleasure
So much of the misery
Like a cyst that swells
The experience when most real
Is nothing short of overwhelming
A dialectical flood of heaven and hell

But here's the thing
I don't think my mom really gets

That love and hate are honestly not separate
We cannot hate without
Ever having deeply cared
Like how love can't be maintained unless
Along the way
You feel scared
If there was nothing
To love, need, or covet
I wouldn't bother to express my hate
If there was nothing
To rush to show up for
I would never be late
Without hope, without trust
Disappointment doesn't exist
Without demands or pressure
There'd be nothing to resist

Without bloody wounds, restraints, or an abscess
No one would ever feel reprieve, relief, or bliss
And confinement, fear, and torture
Make way for freedom, bravery, and grit
One cannot let go without the smallest grasp
Loss just a myth
if it was impossible to last

I cannot hate what I never knew
Never touched nor longed for
At times I dream
Of what I've never dared before
I imagine a sweet symphony
Ill-equipped to picture what was in store

Believe me when I say, scream,
I've tried not to care
I've tried so hard to hold my gaze despite
The blinding glare
I've tried to be
A duck on a pond
Enjoying the spring shower
Letting the beads of water be

As they make their natural way
Down my back, along my layered feathers till
Joining the pool below seamlessly
In a way where no one reacts or retracts
The ripples beautifully unfolding just barely
With a stillness

I regret to lack
But
I'm more like
A duck on a pond
Presenting pristine with little webbed feet
Fighting with fury
Beneath what you can see
I'm the ugly duckling
With ruffled feathers running amok
Randomly between leaves and lily pads
Waves push me till I'm stuck
Loosened roots wrangle my limbs pulling
Me into a game of tug-of-war
While fallen petals buoy on the surface
My heart and lungs get sore
I quack boldly aloud
At matted knots my beak plucks
Causing others to hesitate as if
Passing high-speed Mack trucks

I trail haphazardly behind
The rest of the dutiful line
Getting distracted by that one
Glimmer of light off to the side shining
Sublime
The impermanent reflection of the sun
Beams
Against the liquid concentric circles
That only exist in the moments

Before they by necessity fade
Are like my aspirations and intentions
That life or I

Somehow repeatedly evade or
Erase
Then shy away in disgrace

I hate
Because I've known what it's like to be held
To be on the brink of comfort
To have wished to have hope
To have believed when others lied
About my worth
I hate
Because I was urged to reach out
And as I fell from the cliff
I was told not to slouch
I hate
The empty invitations
Followed by taken seats
Leaving me to fill the random corners
Like an off-brand grout

I hate
When I sit hungry
In view of a buffet
I hate
When I meant to be lovable
But my mind made me

Act another way

I hate
When hugs were held
With robots and con-men
I hate
When my limits, my needs
Were mistaken for burdens

Love like loss
Taunts me daily
Like my will it sustains
And also fails me

The taste of its sweetness
Still sits on my lips
But in the back of my throat
Persistently lingers
A bitterness

#2

I know a lot of things
    but not much
    meaningful
a lot of people know my name or
    whatever they've been told
    in passing, nearly

no one knows my soul
    maybe by design or by default
    safety first, children
I get confused myself by
    who or how or what I am
    where I'm going, all
I know is where I've been
    what I've done
    what others have told me
sometimes I smile, more often
    I grimace, I scowl
    When told to be more becoming
I project my heart
    I clasp my fists around
    something, or nothing
you, you will
    only know
    parts of me
if you happen to be so unlucky
    if you stumble upon the opportunity
    when you were headed elsewhere
if you wander off the beaten path
    away from popular tourists' scenes and
    past signs that warn of mountain lions and bears
if you happen to catch a glimpse
    when I'm not overshadowed by the company of those that
look
    like the pictures you know from glossy magazines
if you're brazen enough to
    withstand my sharp tongue and

don't mind the threads unravelling at the seams
or the semi-healed scabs
I compulsively pick
till they bleed
or the smeared mascara exacerbating
my naturally dark circles
I hate almost as much as myself

or my past
or the future they say is
up to me
I'm told I'm human but
different than whomever
you've met before me
passion fueled by potential
I leave both the gas on
and the tap running

#3

I
I am
Or I never was
I was dragged here
I run when you'd pause
I did
I do, don't, don't want to

I'm not, I no longer, I never knew
I don't know what is, or
What I've got
What you said you think you saw
I never know, or do I
What I'm doing, thinking, feeling
Until I do
You and I together wonder
Where it is I'm heading to
I hide in plain sight
I feel the tension in my jaw
I didn't ask to play this game
I don't abide by your laws
I look for paths to tomorrow
I don't remember
Where I parked my car
I feel my feet on the ground
I look up at the stars
I lock my gates some days
On others leave them ajar
Often forgetting who I am
And how others are
Stumbling through sideways stories
Continual doubt of what I regard
Then there's you or
Some other vague being
You leave satisfied
And I'm left reeling
I try to plan, try to understand, but

I can only observe what I'm doing, thinking, feeling
My eyes strain to see where I could be
I wish I had a worse memory
Forever flashbacks of where I've been
Until the images singe
Facts stun, burns singe, on potential I hinge
Impulsively I recoil
At the image staring back at me each morning
My reality and dreams like
Water and oil
These persistent pasts and crude realities
They prick and poke
They cut too deep
See
The sheets
Drip red
With blood and sweat
Salty as warm tears
Form puddles crystal clear
As my fears all muddled
Burns sear
Leaving scars
They only ever fade so much
As the skin cells peel
Antiseptics and ragged nails alike sting
No one hears my screams
My cheers or jeers
No one feels my desperate hugs
But claim to see my leers

I reach for crisp sheets
To wrap 'round me tightly
All souls stand alone
Among their peers

POET

Ashley Gaston

Ashley Gaston is a social worker who has earned a B.A. in Psychology from the University of California, Riverside, and an M.Ed. from Arizona State University. She never thought of herself as a writer or shared her poetry publicly until she embarked on a journey of self-discovery. It is on this journey that she was reunited with herself, and consequently, her gift of writing that had long been forgotten. She has never submitted a piece for publication before and is honored to be included in this work from The Poets Underground.

Avatar 7/29/2022

Western civilization
Its culture is cruel
Feeding off our fragmented souls
Essence sucked, parched
Like vampire's bite, blood lost
Our mind jumbled, reprogrammed to mush
How can we survive on this hamster wheel of death?
We're not intended to

Time monetized when it doesn't really exist
A tool to desynchronize life with living
Feeding on our fear
We must break free
Go inwards, find our spirit
Search our souls until there's nothing left to uncover
Break apart, let the light in
Expose the darkness
Find our way back to our roots of Being,
    Not doing, slaving, striving, or fearing
Just breathing. Connecting.
Not to this well-conditioned avatar,
But to who we truly are.

The Journey 8/24/2022

I walk
    through dry basins, hidden by mountain ranges.
    Breathless. Not a cleansing wind alive.
    Sun-cracked grounds, dusted, parched.
I tramp
    through frozen lands. No warmth in sight.
    Frostbite on fingers and toes.
    The world unfelt. Clouded by pain and storm.
I drown
    in murky waters of deep.
    Crashing waves of an overtaking.
    Barely treading currents of unknown.
I crawl
    through deserts of heated despair.
    Blistering past and boiling wound.
    The future a mere mirage. Untrue.
I climb
    mountains of old. Uncovered wisdom.
    Endless toil in search of truth.
    Scratching, clawing through the distance.
I reach
    the summit of a pinnacle,
    where I am meant to be.
I jump
    into the air of uncertainty,

    fueled by faith and fear, simultaneously.
I fly
    among the sister clouds.
    Soaring in the bliss and synchronicity.
    A knowing that everything for me,
    waits in the wind and clouds in the sky
    of Ascension.

Entangled 9/2/2022

The unfolding.
Releasing remnants of the past,
    like bloody entrails from within.
Blood spatter, staining the walls of my soul.
Wretched rejection of patterns of old.
Reveal the stories that keep me cold, lifeless, and numb.
Locked away, bound, heavy ball and chain.
Entangled, held captive.
Slave to the curses.
Release me, let my spirit free,
    to remember who I am meant to be.

POET

Brian T. Meyer

Brian Meyer is a plein air poet and painter of San Diego jazz, known for creating on the spot at local clubs and concerts. His words and art arise from these moments; a practice based on Jazz, improvisation, developing chops outside any comfort zone, and always asking; does it swing? A native San Diegan, US Army Veteran, and San Diego Watercolor Society member.

the Master

do you remember him
that noble teacher
a master swordsman
his craft his art
his skill and knowing
of such renown
the students came from all around
he challenged them to show their worth
he taught them his real art
but as lessons
only he could learn
never catering to second rate
each tried and failed
they died before his blade
long gone now forgotten
all he knew lost
a master with no one
to remember

Recycled Words

in reading recycling
I scavenge my writing

the discards I am hoarding
this junkyard of wording

an Earnest Moveable Feast
of Chaucer Joyce and Yeats

such wealth to coin a word
such nonsense is heard

without meaning
just noise to annoy

limits of vocabulary
dictionaries define
your limits of mind

your limits of thinking
limit my meaning

these steampunk frankensteins
the debris of Shelley
Stoker and Verne

I repurpose into verse
this junkyard of wording
in a world that stopped reading
poems I am hoarding

here on the street

late monday past midnight
down 5th and island
by the tipsy crows door
the line waits to join in
each drink an escape
from this world
we are in

across the street
long after last call
when the party is gone
tired bar maids remain
to sweep out the lonely
whiskey girls floor

down on the street
an elder lies there
in his piss in the gutter
done begging to live
drinking to him
the way to exist

the bars empty out
their liquid courage
stumbles back home
into ubers
refusing to be see
these living debris

here on the street
there is a beat
and then
there are the beaten
no one lets in

POET

Brooke Gerbers

Brooke started out their poetry career in 2019 as a spoken word artist, after being introduced to the slam poetry community in San Diego, California. They have since then taken first place in slam poetry competitions, had the opportunity to perform in cities such as Seattle, Las Vegas and Phoenix, as well as use their passion for advocacy and the arts by being a guest speaker at human rights rallies and fundraisers. Brooke has used their poetry to explore queerness, trauma feminism, and other topics we were taught not to speak about at the dinner table. When they aren't on a stage, they're probably lost in the mountains somewhere with a dead car battery and their puppy, Myka, hoping everything works itself out.

The Parts You would have Taken with You (Thank God you Didn't)

My therapist asked what I remembered most.
I said the big corner desk—
You know, the one I'd bring you coffee to each morning while you prepped for your meetings.
She asked how I felt about the desk.
I told her I felt like maybe the wood was always more weathered than we thought,
And that stuffing the drawers with love letters was a silly use of space,
And that when an entire bottle of antidepressants hits the surface all at once, it sounds a lot like a tree fist-fighting a bolt of lightning.

I'd say we were both lucky to have come out of that storm alive.

My therapist asked if the desk still haunts me now.
I said no, but I still search my trash can for pieces of your goodbye letter,
And I still think about the laps that held my head while yours rested in a hospital bed,
And I still wish in the bending of yourself, you spared me the break.

But we didn't know anything about warped wood.

We thought that maybe if we yelled loud enough or long enough,
We could drown out the sound of our carpenter bones buckling under the weight.

They don't tell you that if a tree falls in a forest it doesn't have to make a sound—
That sometimes silence is the loudest house guest.

For what it's worth, I am glad you finally found the hammer and nails and have started making noise again during your reconstruction.
That desk always was your most prized possession.

Steps to Making a House a Home:

- Hide the empty whiskey glasses behind the smiles in the family portrait that hang above the mantle
- Stop setting out 4 plates at dinnertime
- Start only pouring 3 glasses of milk
- Memorize which one of the stairs creaks (3rd) and how much time you have to rub the sleep from your eyes and prepare your shaking fists (20 seconds)
- Pick out a plot of land in the cemetery out back
- Spray paint your name in the grass, right there
- Stick a post-it note on the wall in every place he calls you "bitch"
- Make a maze out of these hallways so there are plenty of places to hide
- Or vantage points to attack from
- When it finally starts to feel more air than cage, move
- Repeat

Between Slab City and Salvation

I wonder how many people have walked away thinking that I am the most broken place they've ever been—

If they took one look at my crooked rib cage
Barely guarding my blue-tarp'd heart
And saw that what appeared to be a welcome sign,
Was actually a warning.
That there is no electricity to keep us warm here,
And the lack of a front door makes it easy to leave without making a sound.
If they saw that the road between my splintered floorboard feet and shoes to protect theirs stretched for miles,
Or that I'd crafted a bed out of scrap metal and things I wish I would have said
Would they think to themselves:
How could anyone make a home here?

I wonder how many people have walked away thinking that I am a masterpiece—

If they took one look at the shattered windows and knew I just wanted to let the light in,
And saw what appeared to be just shards of glass,
Were actually the wind chimes that sang them to sleep.
If they held onto these rusted radiator hands
And found that they still gave off enough heat to keep theirs warm too,
Or that the kitchen table was held up by all of the times I begged for an exit route,
But forced these legs to go a few more miles instead
Would they think to themselves:
Would she let me make a home here too?

POET

Casey Cariño

"I've been writing off and on for about ten years to help me figure out what I'm feeling during times I didn't know who to talk to. I hope in sharing my thoughts, something resonates with you and you'll feel a little less alone."

- C.C.

Drunk, diluted, and dissociating

6 shots to unmute the silence
13 shots to make the curious brave enough
19 shots to knock me out
22 - make it hurt less
25 - make it all go away
26 - praying to an unknown god for a miracle:
"Something good has to happen. It has to."

But I'll pour enough coke to dilute the sting and ignore the burn
To blissfully comply with ignorance of the severity I just consumed.

I might've chased the taste away
But there's a buzz in my head that some Tylenol cannot ease.

Maybe if I don't acknowledge it - it won't exist.

It's like a buzzing light in a waiting room;
It doesn't exist until the lights go off and now it's silent but it's also dark now and (in this scenario) everyone has left the building.

Maybe if I close my eyes and become as quiet as this setting
None of the problems exist.
But that doesn't take me out of the building.

6 steps back - do I really want to leave?
13 steps forward - I'm not sure where I'm going.
19 steps back - there's comfort in the familiar.
22 steps back and forth - maybe I can do both.
25 steps just going in circles - wasting breath I barely have.
26 steps towards the exit - I'm not sure where it'll go, but it's not here;
And that has to be better.

Uproot and undo

I should have done this sooner
I should have figured it out long ago
  But now I'm racing the clock
  And there's a hint of insincerity -
  A questionable doubt.
I should have known by now.
Now I'm scrambling,
My head's scrambled
Thoughts like pieces of Scrabble
No letters really matter, no words -
Just word vomit.
I take what is needed and create what I want -
If only I had a breath of clarity.
Some way to decipher what is feeling versus
  thought to relieve the churning in my chest
  and to catch oxygen in my lungs - I feel...
Like I'm running out.
Running out of steam
Out of drive,
Running out of reason to continue to survive
  what I don't understand.
I'd rather uproot than untangle the roots
  that entangle me and strangle me;
I've let them grow too long.
I should have done this sooner.

Crumbs

I thought the crumbs I was fed was a feast;
No one said I could sit at the table.

So I begged for scraps and thanked you for it.

The smallest drops spilled over gave me reprieve, it was the sustenance that kept me alive - so who was I to reject your morsels when they began to rot?

I knew nothing else, I needed to live.

So I kept begging,
    And eating,
    And crying,
    And thanking you for your crumbs.

If I asked for more, you'd act out in rage - I was selfish for wanting what others barely had
So I shut my mouth while the scraps were saved and shipped away.

Later I discovered the droppings you let fall were the result of your greed - too busy holding on for yourself

I took what I could get and it became me that was rotting.

Until I crowned myself with a thought -
Smaller than your crumbs
Comparable to seeds
And learned to harvest a bounty.

POET

Chris Ernest Nelson

Chris Ernest Nelson, a graduate of San Diego State University, is a retired high school history and art teacher. His history of the 1939 election contest over food-stamps for the elderly, "The Battle for Ham and Eggs", appears in the Journal of San Diego History, Fall 1992. He was named Author of the Month (November 2018) by the San Diego Public Library for his book "HARVEST the poetry of Chris Ernest Nelson". Find all of his poetry at: chrisernestnelson.wordpress.com

Carry It All to the Altar

Life is a gathering together of thoughts and feelings:
the longings, the waitings, the voices, the touches;
the casual greetings, and the grinding goodbyes.
Nothing is wasted, everything is accounted and saved.

I carry it all to the altar.
I make a sacrifice of tears.
I make a sacrifice of longing.
I make a blood sacrifice.

Every day I count my misdeeds and my triumphs,
in a nexus moment of contrition and celebration.
I know everything has happened according to plan.
I know all my days have served this sacred purpose.

I carry it all to the altar.
I make a sacrifice of song.
I make a sacrifice of laughter.
I make a willing sacrifice.

Chris Ernest Nelson 2022

POET

Chris Vannoy

He came out of the Kansas prairie to grow up in the California sun. Poetry is his passion. Voicing it, his art.

Sky Ride

Gripping the handles
Of his ejection seat
Clinching his jaws,
Planting his feet
Roaring engines
Assail his ears
Heart beats count
The minute-years
Gravity crushes him
In his chair
Flaming his chariot
Leaps to the air
Booster rockets
Kick in and then
It's off from his star-home
Once again.

I'll Do It Tomorrow

I'll do it tomorrow
... put up the cloths
...fix the broken fence
... change the oil in the car

I'll do it tomorrow
... it's gotten to hot
   to pull weeds
   ... mow the lawn
   ... crawl up in the attic
      and splice the cable
      into the computer room

I'll do it tomorrow
... yes,
   I know that's what I said YESTERDAY,
   But I WILL ...

I'LL DO IT TOMORROW!

Ybor City

the drunk beside me eases
one nickel and two dimes
onto the counter
making sure he doesn't miss
as the vinegar the bar maid just sloshed on the fish and chips
invades my nostrils

I take a sip of my first East Coast Cappuccino
taste the hot and whip cream
There is nothing else for me
here at Albie's.

The cigarette smoke burns my eyes

maybe that's why I seldom go to bars
or it could be the loud music
or the incessant clamor of voices
invading my otherwise quiet nature
or the way that women look at me
then look away
not waiting to match my stare

they know I'm going home alone
know that the last few coins
that jingle on the counter
are all I have left.

POET

Christian Gabriel Moro

Christian is an attorney-cum-poet from Sacramento, CA. He has published two chapbooks with Know Good Books: *20 Years of Solitude y Una Canción Desesperada* and *30 Years a Fool*. His forthcoming poetry and prose book, *Papito y Chiquitita*, explores his journey of becoming a father at 20 years of age and again at 34. You can find him online @cgmoro and **cgmoro.substack.com**.

the marlin and me

I spent all year not knowing
how old I am.

Not that I do not know what
year I was born
or what year it currently is but
more that time
has become a marlin in the vast
blue ocean
and I have been living in a tug
boat pulling along a barge
laden with all my brackish
hopes and saline dreams
towards a port eternally just
over the horizon.

The ocean is vast.
I work every day.
The ocean is deep.
I work every day.
There are no tides out here.
There are no waves.
There is only the marlin and
me.

I am 7 years old eating peaches
in the crux
of the old peach tree out back.
I am 17, falling in love over
and over.
I am 37, a father figure still
figuring it out.

I am the captain now.

The fishing rods bob up and
down as they troll behind the
boat. A dorsal fin flashes off in
the distance
as the marlin reminds me it is
still out there.
I feel my age in my bones.
Everything tastes of salt and
tomorrow is such a long time.

Across the still water I hear my
mom calling me in for dinner.
The sun dips below the horizon
and in the penumbra I see
myself setting the table for our
grandkids.

The marlin lives on.

As do I.

mondaze

It is always Monday.
On that, at the very least, we
can most certainly count on.

The years peel off
one by one
as we chip away to get to the
core
of who and why we are.

Some Mondays are birthdays.
Others anniversaries.
Some Mondays languish from
wanting
while others are technicolored
dream coated orgasms of
activity.

My youngest pecks away at her
breakfast dutifully
and has not a clue what day it
might be.
For her, it is always now.
If she wants something, it is
now.
If she loves you, it is now.
If she is sleepy or hungry or
cuddly, it is now.

Her smile is now and her tears
are now.
Now is eternal and there is no
time to waste on naming the
days.
At most, days are used to
delineate

what the letter of the day will be on Sesame Street.

The letter of the day today is M.

M is for Monday.

Frida

My wife leaves me small
works of art in the shower.
Hair is her preferred medium.

Every morning is a Rorschach
test
as I turn the faucet and wait for
the warm water to make its
way through the pipes.

The strands swoop around and
intersect each other at sharp
angles.
They defy gravity plastered up
against the tiles by the
humidity.
They defy god.

I am no art critic.
Far be it for me to judge her
process
or question the truth behind her
artistic vision.

I am just a man.
In a shower.
Standing before a hairball.

And if the true meaning of art
is to bring forth emotion
then these are a compendium
of daily masterpieces.

They initially evoked
annoyance
but through their persistent
presence over the years

they now bring up a fondness
rooted in familiarity.

They tell a story across time.
Their lengths and color belie
the seasons of our life.
The stresses of career and
motherhood affect their
volume.
[The Postpartum Period was
prolific.]

It's Bauhaus with balayage.
Umbra via ombré.
A Louvre of love, if you will.

I feel the water cascade down my back as I lather the shampoo on my head. V QSI breathe in deeply and exhale as the vanity mirror begins to fog up.
Today's piece slowly starts to slide down the tile towards the drain.

POET

Christopher Mohn

Christopher Mohn is an LA based artist who is proficient in various mediums including music, art, and now poetry. Prior to lockdown he was touring internationally as a DJ, however due to lockdown had to stop which allowed for his transition into poetry. He recently self-published a book of poetry and art titled "This Is Love, Infinite" and has begun reading regularly at different poetry readings around the city. Check out his Instagram @christophermohn_artpoet to keep in touch.

My Nightstand Yearns for Change

I've been storing
my fears and my worries
in a honey jar i keep in my stomach
where flies gather and breed
where alley cats pick the flesh off of bones
where manuscripts full of dreams
are thrown out and burned

i remind the sweet lord
i have a bible on my nightstand
next to the reading light
that collects dust on the shade
next to empty water glasses
next to charms
amulets
gemstones
tarot cards
star charts
Buddhist prayers
and a house plant
that's my only friend

I ponder all of these things
and realize that loneliness
is only a misunderstanding
between the heart and soul
and suddenly I feel a little less lonely
as I dip my fingers in the honey jar
and go to sleep

Scrap Paper

the scrap paper on my windowsill
is where falcons nest black clouds
blanketing dragon fire
as I watch the rain
wash the sidewalk clean
I watch the water
wash the ink off the page

this is where I view
my love like a puzzle
finding the edges
to piece the picture together
the impossible task-
skeleton hands
wrap the blindfold tighter
and my heart explodes
with fluid motion
that spins me like a kaleidoscope
changing colors and shapes
changing like leaves on the ground
changing & changing & changing

this is what we are when we pray

Real Warriors

real warriors
don’t carry weapons
or fight wars
or draw first blood
or boast
or conquer

no
the real warriors
are the ones who wake
into their own battles
who are run down in the street
who are cut open and drained
who are broken hearted
& afraid
who are lost
who still find a way
to wake in the morning
& stare death in the face
& walk the path
with golden grace

yes
the real warriors are the ones
all around us
fighting, fighting, fighting
fighting these silent battles
that the world
will never know

POET

Dennis Young

Author of the book, The Ascension Key; Dennis is a thought provoker and creative visionary. Much of his writing style aims to promote connectedness, self-acceptance and authentic expression. He lives by the motto that no voice deserves to be lost in the sea of other narratives.

God

I don't look for God and I don't pray to a Czar in the sky
I'm not waiting for heaven in the great beyond when heaven is always nigh
I no longer question my worth, my existence or if I even matter
All the things in my highest good are served to me on a silver platter
I don't search for God in buildings or in certain communities
My eyes are wide, and I have to tell you about the God I see
I see God when I wake up and look into the mirror
I glance into my soul to see myself much clearer
God is all around me as I'm walking through the park
And I meet God passed out on the sidewalk covered in her track marks
I get to feel God's presence when dining with friends and family
I always take a little extra to go in case I see God hungry
God is exalted, grand, expansive, pure and heightened
God is the little boy hiding under his bed cause dad's home and he's frightened
God is my homeless friend Phil sitting and seeking help from above
God gives us opportunities to relate to ourselves and reconnect in love
I see God in the way nature is drawn to me
I see God in the twinkling eye of that curious little baby
I see you God sitting in front of me comfy in your chair
I feel you God in pain feeling like everyone else is unaware
I love you God and thank you for being such diversity
Thank you, God, for being with me right now in this part of reality

Healing Journey

How do we begin to heal the earth
What if we started with laughter and mirth
Respected each other's spaces and features
Not just humans but all earth's creatures
To share and cohabitate this place we call home
To not cut down, develop and every square inch own
We don't have to respond to every emotional situation
Instead let's spend our energy on the magick of creation
We owe nothing to no one and that's such a relief
As we grow we can vanquish our old childhood beliefs
What if we stopped taking ownership of past inflicted trauma
And broke free from cycles of internalized drama
What if we knew we are God and stopped hating that name
If we knew ourselves more clearly could we let go of blame
We can call it Jehovah, Lucifer, Buddha, Allah, Kali or just energy
The terminology is not as important as realizing we are that divinity
Should we stop blaming groups, individuals and everything outside
And search within to see where the misery hides
What if we could indulge without the need to escape or cover
If we partook in pleasures from a healed space how much more could we discover
What if we stopped foraging for problems and all our worries quit rehearsing
Can we really overhaul our lives with our thinking and our versing
Do you think a shift in perspective could shift our experience instantaneously
What if we could heal without having to make it a lifelong journey

Celebrate Men

I love men and no it's not just for sex
I respect men and their essence; I hate to see you vexed
We too have had our voices stolen
By an ancient narrative to which many are still beholden
We are taught we must over-talk, overtake, rule and dominate
Play your role in society or you they will alienate
Everyone wants an idea of what they think masculinity is all about
So, we cripple our feminine component and drown our truest expressions out
Some might say here we go making excuses for men
But we all were duped into thinking we are either masculine or feminine
We are both and must embody with balance if we hope to heal and grow
When truly actualized beings meet the magick starts to flow
Our misalignment has caused destruction, pain and much chagrin
But still, I will always uplift, encourage and celebrate men
See we don't have to diminish men for women to be equal
We can cut that narrative, redefine ourselves and write a new sequel
I won't attack or belittle you because you're straight and white
No matter your skin tone or orientation, man, you are everything right
I love your energy, the way you think and all your many features
You are good, healthy, necessary, capable creatures
I love the way you love and how you throw yourself all in
I hope you start to love and cherish yourself and see your value from within
You are not just a paycheck, moral and financial support
You are the Sun, the Moon, the Cosmos and every truth they try to thwart
Beautiful man come back to yourself overthrow the narrative and win
I don't care who you are or what you've done, I will always celebrate men

POET

Gabriela Blaszko

Born and living in Poland, started writing in 2016. On a daily basis studies English Philology and works on developing writing skills. With a cup of tea and rock playing in headphones, turns reality into poetry.

Poem 1:

When You cry behind closed door
And only stars are watching,
Your heart is sore
And tears from your eyes are dropping
You fall asleep, tired of life
No dreams in your head appear
That's when your mind
Calms all your aches
And for a brief time, your head is clear
Sun wakes you in the morning
Or moon lets you see the dawn
Either way you are awake now
And you realize that it's gone
All the sadness you were feeling
All the "friends" that end up leaving
Insecurities you've made up
After all, you get to stand up
You gather the strength
To look in the mirror
Clearly seeing the face there showing
You've known it since you can remember
But eyes are slightly different
Looking closely, you realize
That's the glimpse of hope glowing
That means not all is lost
And your heart is still beating
Although that the life is a circle
Steering wheel needs drivers gripping.

Poem 2:

My heart has never been broken
But I can't tell for sure
It's certainly still beating
But what if it has been fooled
It sought for love
Where there was none
And made a place
For what is gone
I think it's been in pieces
From the very beginning
Because how can you not give at least a piece
For everything that has meaning
It's hard to keep together those parts
Without a soul to put them in
Truly one of the finest arts:
To complete the puzzle, you must begin
Since every beginning has its end
If my life ever won't be able to extend
Full of memories, people and words ever spoken
I hope that my heart will stand with its truth
An remain unbroken.

Poem 3:

The truth is a lie more times than you think
Beauty fades with age
Wide street is a dead end
And time flies as you blink
You are lost in directions
Although you go only forward
From the brave adventurer
What's left is only coward
All the bridges are burning
You left nothing but ashes
So nobody could find you
While your hope silently crushes
Are you proud of what you did?
Killed the spark that lit the way
Convinced yourself that what you got
Is everything you'll ever need
No matter how deep you'll burry yourself
No matter how good you will hide the truth
When you spent so much time in the darkness
It starts to speak to you.

POET

Hilary Charlene Broman

Hilary's passion for writing started at the age of 11 and she has been writing ever since. She finds joy in sharing her work and believes that poetry is one of the most authentic ways to connect with others. You can contact her and find more of her work on Instagram @hilarycharlene.

Six Years Tomorrow

You are the room, the building, the event that brought the crowd
your followers who you love to let love you
they are close enough for me to taste
their sweat on your lips, their salt in our bed
your thoughts in their head.

I am pushing past you in a crowded room
holding my breath, squeezing toward the exit.
You spill yourself into the spaces I need to breathe,
to cool, to gather the bits of me being kicked around by shuffling feet.

I am yours to make small, to half
then to quarter
to place in your back pocket and to forget
to lose, to let fall
into old spilt beer and stick to the bottoms of shoes
your shoes,
your show.
I watched on repeat
ruined myself just to leave.

Now I spill in my dreams into my mother's lap and wake
alone in a pile of me.
My salt.
My bed.
My thoughts
finally not yours in my head.
I woke up without you next to me.
I woke up without you next to me for the first time in years
six years tomorrow.

I woke up without you
and I woke up without you
and I woke up without you
until I woke up from you.

Something Real

I want to be more than someone you scroll past/ I want face to face laughter and cracked pepper in your teeth/ cold fumbling hands making their way into my pockets and up my sleeves/ goosebumps rising like little suns across the sky we share/ you and I glowing there/ I want nerves/ I want wild and rare/ real in a world where real is fading/ I want staying that doesn't feel like staying.

Fruit for Breakfast

She's an early riser.
Kisses my cheek before the sun has a chance to. Nudges me into the still dark morning with her playful hands, she finds and wakes the lost parts of me. I was a dreamer before I learned how to sleep through anything. She doesn't remember her dreams at all so she makes them up as she goes. Today it's us on an empty beach before sunrise, it's our sand covered hands sticky from the first bite of the soft, sweet day.

POET

JAck STuart SMith

"Singing my songs at County Mental Health. Behavioral Health volunteer to Marines and their families, including sharing my songs on Suicide Prevention Days. Father of three children, one special needs with CP. Built a "Talking Circle" at our home, to reach out to the community, my wife Loni and I, giving space to those who have, "Things Left Unsaid." Supporter at Sundance in Arizona. Was told by oncologist in 2014, "Get your things together, you have a year and a half to live." Singer/songwriter, loving writing poetry, to uplift and stir, hearts and minds."

- J.S.S.

There Are Designs

All,
is intentional,
by design,
made to fit,
harmoniously.

There is a beauty,
the heart can sense, and,
eyes are made to see with,
wondrous spiritual clarity.

A natural fit,
puzzle pieces,
joined to perfection,
to form this surreal scene.

Let us join our hands,
every finger entwined,
like the roots of a great banyan tree,
growing together,
no one root,
more important than the other.

All,
are pieces and a part,
of the entirety,
every molecule.

Every tear,
and all laughter,
flows into the same basket,
woven by the gods,
held and remembered for eternity.

May we walk in forbearance and grace,
may we learn to resonate together,
In harmony,

may we form a chain of healing,
never letting one link be forgotten.

We are here to join our family,
there is only one family.
Our family's name is Life,
and all that exists,
are precious relatives.

Intricate,
snowflakes and crystals,
are formed without,
a human hand.
Miracles like these,
formed us as well,
after all,

There Are Designs.

JAck STuart SMith

These Things, I Know, You May Never Understand

I told you I would always love you,
till the day I died.
You said you would laugh on that day.

I understand you,
I know you very well.
Sometimes you don't mean the things you say,
and you quite often change your mind,
regretting words that were spoken.

It's an emotion,
deep inside my heart.
When I get near you,
the hollowness in my soul cries out.

Special,
you are so very special,
I know this,
I held you,
the day you were born,
my star, my angel, my sweet one.

You will most likely never read this,
regardless though,
I send healing energy your way,
be well always.

You are young,
the world is large and overwhelming,
I love you with all my life.

These things,
I know,
you may never understand.

JAck STuart SMith

Pick Beautiful Flowers

Sad,
be this shadow,
confusion's firm grasp,
taking hold.

The darkest abyss,
seems like springtime.
A breath of fresh sunshine,
and fire.

Tunnels, dampness and dregs
If light be lost, travel I darkly, deeply
Good fortune, my will to prevail residing
A denizen, looking past heavy iron gates

Much of this gloomy shadow, carry I
The nature of this human beast, angelic
Ambiguousal heart, sweet innocent child, I
Walk as if this place were my own, and

Pick Beautiful Flowers

JAck STuart Smith

POET

James Rauff

James Rauff is a Los Angeles based artist and creator of Recirculation Art. His works reflect his background in history combined with his intrigue and interpersonal relationships.

Luca (Reprise)

It's all digital now
From the gift of gab
To the grift and grab
There used to be an
Art to this
You indexed champion
You faux fox
With too many skins on the wall
When the hunts so easy
The taxidermy is less deserving
You still smell like fawn
Haven't even learned how to run

We don't disappear
We are tagged like animals
Left a digital trail
Migrated to me
So symptomatically
Arthritic intentions
You got in the rhythm
Advertised to you
Based on consonant
I'm in your algorithm
We have our discourses
Buttoned up
Lectured lovers
So
Touch me or don't

“Haley Jobe”

(Western Texas)
Someone needs to crank up the topography
We need to get higher
Above the Edward and Stockton plateaus
So, we can scream into these comatose canyons
Wake up some hitch-hiked hearts
Be the breeze to this tumbleweed lifestyle
Because something has to be the propellant
A voice behind the telethon
Because out here it echoes like cathedrals
And we don’t have a prayer in this heat
It’s even hot for arsonist
So, let’s burn it up

(Eastern Long Island)
Light pollution westward and upward
We need to get higher
Eastbound toward Montauk Point
So, we can seam together an escape plan
From the Hampton highfalutin hearts
Be the tidal wave to this whitewash
Because gravity is an anchor
A rhythmic voice in the night
Making the ebb and flow inevitable
And we would sink if not for its retreat
It’s even dizzying for the buoys
So, let’s turn this light down

1.0
(Via Batteries Not Included)

Life has increased its toll to keep up with inflation
And we are showing our age
All of our faith in the future is tied to annuities
Ideology can be fleeting
Praying to a neon God
His light is always on
Toggle switch desires
I can turn it off whenever I like
Technology or Old Testament
There has got to be A new name on the Marquette
Jesus just isn't a draw anymore
Turn water into liquid crystal
Turn photos into faith

POET

Jane Muschenetz

Poets Underground Headliner (6/2022), Jane Muschenetz debuted many of the poems in her first collection of poetry, "All the Bad Girls Wear Russian Accents" (Kelsay Books, 2023) at the Acid Vault. Check out her award-winning prose and art @PalmFrondZoo and www.PalmFrondZoo.com

For Sunny Rey & Anthony Azzarito at the Acid Vault
After Opening for the Poets Underground

Open Mic

Knock, Knock!—Open Up!
(It's OK, let it in)

Let it in, let it out,
Open
your mouth, breathe…
Open
yourself to what *could* be
Open
your heart,
Open
your mind—Open Sesame

Each of us is a key
so, take your turn,
Open
whatever door you like,
Open
the palm of your hand—

Here's the mic

"[When people] had all one language... they said, 'Let us build a tower to the heavens, let us make a name for ourselves' ...God saw and said, 'Behold...they have all one tongue, and this tower is only the beginning of their ambition... Let us confuse their language, so that they may not understand one another..." Therefore, it was Babel, for the people no longer spoke the same tongue and dispersed over the earth." *-Genesis 11:1-9*

Babel

Remember when we all, collectively, agreed
that we should eat > 5 servings of fruits & vegetables daily?
It meant something, that common ground
even if, in the end, we all ate uncomplicated carbs instead.

Also, daily walks! Also, fresh air!
Also, birds & relationships & meaningful work &
Love!/Un-loneliness!/Good Deeds!/*Gratitude!*/ Also—
BREATH ......even......slow......deep.....

And yeah, maybe, we didn't believe in *God* the same way,
but we did share a sense of what was good
a common aspect, articulating some unifying love
of *"Motherhood & Apple Pie,"* all of us
pulling our own bootstraps in one direction—up!
(toward heaven) like a multilingual prayer

our words, unhinging, from the dictionary's wooden thud,
swarming into flight, like bees abandoning the hive collective–

Things That We Speak / Things That Remain   Unspeakable

within us, honeycomb husks of truth and hope
still sweet and waxing on our tongues...

Remember what we said
we'd taste instead?

First published: *The Decadent Review,* Dec 2021

For those of us forced to flee

the world is forever shrinking down to a single question:
What can you carry?
The suitcase of your heart closed tight
on all the things there was no room to bring--
your memories of "home," the snowflake moments
of your youth, the blooming Lilac tree
outside your bedroom window... a heavy burden
saps your strength on the long journey, bring
only what you need.
Homes can be built again,
a new tree can be rooted.

Survive.

When you have nothing left to plant, become the seed.

First published: *The Good Life Review,* 2022 Honeybee Poetry Prize Winner

POET

Jason Noble

To make a proper Jason Noble: Mix one third cup redneck, one half pint hipster, add a pinch of poetry, a teaspoon of education, a shot of tequila, a midlife crisis and a sprinkle of sarcasm. Then take a dollop of coconut oil, massage until hard, and bake for 48 years. Drizzle with some quick wit and spit and serve with a side of fuck this shit.

Dwindling Embers

I want to paint you a picture.
So, picture, if you will
a stump.
Its old, hard and mossy covered trunk rests beside a river, in a slow, de-compositional phase.
It's cut off about three feet up from where it used to grow in glory, previously shading a flat and sandy spot, just above the bank in a slow swirling bend of a small and rocky river way up in the Blue Ridge mountains of Appalachia, somewhere in northern Georgia.
Humans have camped and fished and fucked and hunted and died here for thousands of years.
I myself have swum and waded and gleefully tossed round smooth skipping stones over rapids and into waterfalls and jumped from high rock cliffs into shallow swimming holes and fucked and frolicked in and around this ancient wooded rocky river for 40 fucking years.
So, on this aforementioned stump, a scene is set - several things are deliberately stuck, stabbed and stacked: a shiny and sharp wood-handled camping hatchet, a large bowie knife made of Pakistani steel, a set of extra-long cooking tongs, a half smoked blunt, and a large bottle of over-proofed dark Caribbean rum, mostly full.
Now, some folks might think of such a purposely constructed scene as easy and aggressive, maybe even juvenile, and I wouldn't disagree.
It took me a few minutes to set it all up, complete with the bend in the river background, for the purpose of exercising some stoned and drunken creative demons during an impromptu Instagram photo shoot.
I considered titling it, fittingly, "implements of destruction".
However, as I gazed upon the results, I had a realization of the possibilities and even the inevitabilities of creation in this scene,
as if with a sperm and an egg
or a big bang
or a puddle of primordial ooze
When you think about the possibilities that could come out of this concoction, they become overwhelming and almost endless, and on this night the following things came to mind:
A killer buzz

a gaping head wound
some well-made food
a life story
a love story
a marriage
a divorce
a slit throat's blood splashing and spilling onto the sand
like a small stream in the silver moonlight
a poem
an anthology
the glory and finality of revenge after years of personal terror and
abuse
a nightmare
a child
a nightmare child
a card table flipped over in anger
the worst hangover since that morning after that bachelor party in
Tijuana
an ill-advised foray to the swimming hole on a dark poison ivy trail
with nothing but a horror movie flashlight
a story
a fable
a splinter pulled from a lion's paw
a fireside confession of a past indiscretion
a rough carving of a demigod drunkenly hacked into the trunk of a
dead tree
an angry spasm that results in bodily harm
a Viking funeral
a bludgeoning
some dirty hot and sweaty tent sex while grasping and sliding inside
a questionable sleeping bag
a bug-bitten genital
a blood orgy
that last round of shots you probably shouldn't have had
a cry for help
a door of perception that opens into the subconsciousness of one's
mind
an endless war based on an old family feud
a frying pan full of bacon
a broken bone

a busted knee
a hacking cough
a meteor strike
a stolen election
a pandemic
a hickey from a hillbilly
the blood of one's enemies
and the ability to make fire
But most likely this night will end
in a slow sideways drift
off of life's short
and steep
bittersweet cliff
while I camp
beside this ageless river
and slide deep
into the dying
and dwindling embers
of this campfire tonight
beside which I sit
and stare
and dream
and write

Firewood Fantasies (Dulzura)

How you feeling?
I’m sitting on my new log bench
staring at the stars
I just got a bonus at work
There’s 5 things on my wish list
The first three:
A chainsaw
A banjo
And a loveseat
It's pretty peaceful out here
In the evenings an amazing sunset peaks between the trees
and beckons me for a better view
So I crack open a Mexican beer that’s made just down the street
and stroll over to the other side of the road
It's more open to the sky over there
So I list fully gaze upon pink ridges sprinkled with scrub
and studded with glowing orange boulders the size of houses
while the coyotes start yipping and yapping
and the local hounds start baying and barking back and forth
in an endless Dulzura dog war
At night the stars come out like a daydream
and the moon weeps shadows across the gurgling stream
In the morning the bees gorge on the pepper trees
their green low hanging blossoming branches
drape the driveway in a tunnel of buzz
In the spring Clouds of pollen float from the pines
their sprouting combs spout yellow dust
that in the gusts
becomes a golden blizzard
The barn owl’s hoot
and the screech owl’s screech
communicating like flying nocturnal predatory dolphins
mating in the trees
in between eating mice and rabbits and moles
while the frogs and toads’ burps and chirps
echo up and down Marron Valley Road
So yeah

out here
Life
is a little different
There's firewood to be gathered and split
and a fire to be lit
in a fireplace in front of which we now gather
and leisurely sit
My poetry is a log
an axe
a wheelbarrow
some sturdy work gloves
some paper
some dry kindling and a match
My moment of Zen is a belt sander
a palm sander
a paint brush
some raw wood and a pint of polyurethane
My meditation is changing out the propane
installing a washer or a dryer or a stove
My relaxation is raking and sweeping the fallen leaves twigs pine needles pinecones and whatever detriment has dropped from last night's windy storm
With fingerless gloves I dance in step to the rhythms of this dry jungle with live oaks and pepper trees and lodge pole pines
With stained overalls and worn-out hiking boots I march along the gravel paths beside gardens and industrial sized storage containers and mini trailers
A part of my old city self has been washed away
The hunger for nightly interactions
and random dive bar conversations
has been satiated and burned away by a warm bright night fire and the cold moonlight as I gaze up at the heaving heavens
Hoping
that One day
a fully fueled and recently sharpened chainsaw
will magically materialize
and fall from the night sky
Into my arms
And thereby fulfill
My firewood fantasies

POET

Jeanette Jaramillo

Jeanette (aka Jenny) is a visual and floral artist, arts advocate, and writer living in Bankers Hill. Prior to moving to San Diego in 2012, she studied studio art, sociology, and the humanities. A fan of Beat poetry, these are her first published poems.

The Time That It Occurred

Maxwell Parish is in the light of the room
Pending your near vision
We work on sides
Who are you? Where next?
I'm right here
Waiting beneath a high sky
And it hasn't slowed down
    Coalescence
    Fusion or not
    Perhaps utter separation
My eye opens
As the other one shuts
Can you hear me?

    - Jeanette E. Jaramillo

breaking him open

I break him open
    No dust comes out
He is like a metal neo icon
Soon every approach demands
    symbolic sense
Free from junk
    no concrete metaphors scream.

- Jeanette E. Jaramillo

Breaking it Bad

Addiction, longing, and greed
Hear our mortality & freedom
Sewing losses and letting go
Holy national borders
fill the trade demand
Consumption dualities!
Fringe suburbia normalcy
Clean intelligence strategy
Oh betrayal, death controls.

- Jeanette E. Jaramillo

POET

Jennifer Karp

Jennifer Karp is a hard-working poet holding a degree in Literature with emphasis on Medieval, Myth, and Legend, from The American University in Washington, DC. Her poems have appeared in over 100 countries in international publications; however, she does not submit her work often. She finds inspiration from world events, and the fragile, beautiful nature of the human condition.

Monday Night Sports

that first punch connects
nose cracks

husband stands over me
closed fist dangling

my own warm blood drips
from his knuckles

swollen cherry red
domes

the salty metal taste of it
the brine of it

browning on my white cotton shirt
like rust

his lips mouth something
like a dying fish

gasping for air
I lean into

the zip of adrenalin
buzzing like a bee
like a chainsaw

and stand-up shaking
like thin thistle in the breeze
flower and weed

round two

because fuck him

Jennifer Karp, 2022

Señora Diabla

con su fruto de útero
en su espalda
no más espacio para ella
Señor.
En lugar de un brillante
estrella
en lugar de una presencia virgen
para elevarla,
Señor
ahora duerme con el diablo
el diablo drena su sangre de vida
mientras ella lleva todo
el peso

Mrs. Devil

with her child
on her back
no more space for her
Mr.
Instead of a shiny
star
instead of a virgin presence
to uplift her,
Mr.
now sleeps with the devil
devil drains his life blood
while she carries all
the weight

Jennifer Karp 2022

The Dance

Dance mijá dance
the men look down
at their guitars
not at your skirts
of fire. They pluck the steps
your feet stomp
the notes
your body becomes
the strings
all around
you fuse with the sound

morse code of the steps
satellites
a comet
revolutions around the sun
fire

Jennifer Karp 2022

POET

K.R. Morrison

While she's currently on a writing sabbatical in a hideaway she calls "Mermaid Town," K.R. Morrison is a San Francisco poet, drummer, and high school teacher who has been teaching English and Creative Writing for 17 years. Her first chapbook ***Cauldrons*** was published by Paper Press Books. Morrison has featured for various podcasts and curations, and she is a Pushcart nominee for her poem, "Her Altar."

Pirate's Nest

inside weekends, you and me
	submerged in water beds

dressed in red silk sheets, maple wood
	guarding our weary heads

a living room alive with rifles on racks, saddle
	exhibits, no teacups or flower vases

you nailed dry roses face down, wild
	yellow dreamcatchers shrined

with red tips hiding love tales
	dead of thirst, arid red secrets

Saturday night was for house chores
	soundtracked by lowrider Motown

we danced we sang, our lungs wrapped
	around *Love Child*

a kind of diary cry between mother
	and daughter, the story of us two

		use newspaper to clean glass
		t-shirt scraps for what's oak, Babygirl

we dusted off looming goodbyes, Sunday
	is coming with its submarine gut souvenirs

Moon time mornings, I watched you sleep
	our dog Red Baron standing guard, beside me

we both absorbed you, finally at rest
    your gold hair and arrowhead cheekbones

guarded by hand carved Harley Davidson wings
    I tried to teleport into your dreams

Stay with me, Momma
one more night

far away from Sunday
    only Pirate Mom and me in her nest

The InSaints

to the InSaint

a Saint in their allegiance
to artists rabid, ruthless
in revolution
by microphone, wild pen, loud paint

to the InSaint

insane for her relentless wrestling
with cemetaried living, the civilized
dead who nest inside burning
churches, screaming for scripture that saves

to the InSaint

the bruised, back patched street
protector, policed and caged
their evicted street codes
molested, murdered, arrested

to the InSaint

armed with courage and reason to rescue
the queen hemmed inside his soul
the bold butch unleashing
an honest man from her iron breast

to his Daughter

now a sex worker
her vandalized
bedtime stories trafficked
by a vagrant dad in her underpants

anointed, InSainted – she
dominates, invades men's narrative

that it is *her* body, *not for free*
for her sex always has a price

to the Beaten

with weathered knuckles, those weathered
by fists, the pummeled InSaint who craves
the taste of sour blood in stinging noses, broken
in swollen lips harboring savage words

and feral
unspeakable

secrets

to the Sinner

disappointed in this world's repetition
who basks in dirty water baptisms, hungry
for a wilderness god, for afterlives
where mouths are stitched

with pearls stolen by pirates
where eyes are cataracted
by clouds made by ferocious angels

fallen.

to every Insaint

waging war in a world captured
by tyrants and savage
humans, I hear your fire
from your glittering trenches

I wave your flag
and with every battle

I pledge
my allegiance.

for Marian Anderson
(Aug 13, 1968-Nov 4, 2001)

Before the Come Down

It's a hot July night in New Orleans.
I'm in a punk bar on Decatur Street, known
to nest or spurn, depending on the havoc.
The moon is new and wet, breathing
on sidewalks carved into scars & loud memories

We line the bar like volcano collectives
each one of us vandalized, healing lost, somewhere
outside, fossilized in love quaked concrete
bad childhoods etched in shadow gutters, whispering
into velvet nights that ask the wind to call the shots

For just one night, we peel ourselves off.

Jack Daniels and cocaine have a way of creating
surprises costumed in conversation, an avalanche
of loud exchange that sculpts us into a message.
Sometimes masks are real faces, soundtracked by a jukebox
eager to work for God, unravel riddles, thirsty

to deliver songs like psychic mediums. Suddenly
a ballad hibernating in our bones
comes on, saves us from the sting -

OH, THIS SONG, THIS ONE! THIS SONG IS MINE
someone wails –

It's like this.

When we're a traveler rather than a tourist
we melt into the moments.
We find that burrow that explains why
so often, we always feel so homeless.
For just one night, the world that refuses us
closes and a bar that refuses to close

teams up with the moon's moods, throws out

just the right people, and in the shadow gravity
of the underground we tumble into prophecy.

Every shot, a dark angel's book of revelations.
Every drug, another invitation to unravel
each other, like tangles of tarnished necklaces.
Every sorry soul, a disciple of something.

No one ever writes about this
in those thick traveller guides.
Ripe with all the right restaurants
swamp tours and cemeteries.
Because what everyone in that bar is searching for, isn't a place.
It's a season of living, a secret language
for finding yourself in a lost and found

and realizing, you're home.
Home isn't a place but in the transition –
hidden in a timeless night
portal of possibility
before the come down.

POET

Kelly Bowen

Kelly Bowen (she/her/hers) is a longtime musician turned writer. Her penchant for the stage evolved to performing stories, which spawned publications: speculative fiction - *Bards and Sages Quarterly*; memoir - So Say We All's *The Whole Alphabet*; poetry - *A Year in Ink, Volume 15*, Poet's Underground *Fuck Isolation* and the *San Diego Poetry annual (2020-2021 & 2022-2023)*. Her friends call her relentless, probably because in addition to writing poetry, she is pitching her first novel, writing the second, and in her spare time, throwing pottery and teaching yoga. **Kellybowenarts.com**.

Storm Walls

I girded the walls
Built them high and strong
Stylized after storm surge barriers
Thick, soaring.

You washed against them
Lapped at their bases
I heard the gentle break of your whispered touch
Sat dry and at ease in my haven

The music of your caress was melodious
The walls stalwart
I allowed your song to continue
The waters rose higher

Still, I sat in safety.
I'd built them high enough, I thought
To withstand the gales
Higher than the crests of you

Sitting in the sun, behind my walls
Water cascaded over the top
One quick beating sheet of
Warm and delectable liquid divinity

The quick touch flared the spark
I could feel you again
Feel the pulsing across space
Across the chasm we mutually built

And I craved, even as I tried to deny it
I turned my face to the next wave that crested my walls, relishing.
Each droplet soaked through my skin
Deep into my pores, through the muscles and flesh
Merged with my blood. Seeped into my heart

I felt the synchrony

The heavenly energetic magnetism
Even fraught with your struggle
Like a limb returning to life

I danced with it. A little.
How much water can I allow past my bulwark without drowning me?

And when, like the tide sucks the ocean away
I begin to need the water, to rely on it for sustenance
You'll pull it away, like a parlor trick magician
Leave my walls battered
New cracks in the crusty mud of me as the moisture vanishes
A return to my arid sanctuary

Picking

I am stupid
Picking at the scab as if expecting
What?
A fresh bloom of deliciousness?
No, it oozes and seeps
Without fail
A flash flare of the angst and pain I thought I'd overcome

Instead with roaring clarity
The agony returns as if I have been freshly gouged

And worse still is the knowing.
The knowing what would happen
And doing it anyway

Watching my hands
Slowly and inexorably
Rip the scab
Dig into the flesh
Ferret in the now gaping wound
As if what else would I find
Other than flayed raw nerves
Newly exposed to the air
Screaming in dismay

I pack it with mud
Drown the screams with anything I can find
Slam the lid closed
Though tendrils snake out and wave at me

Ever the fool
Expecting what?
A release from the torture of my own mind?

Dirt Girl

I breathe the words
You inhale the very firmament
I crave to sit in your garden
Watch you hum and dance
An unobserved observer
As if I am simply yet another flower hidden amongst the unharvested bounty

To let the flow percolate from you to me
And out through my fingers into words on a page
And thus, back to you
Words crafted for you, of you, of me and this bizarre synchrony
Otherworldly and unexpected
As rich as the soil you nurture

You climbed inside my skin
But unlike a snake,
I have no desire to slough off this new layer
Instead, I crave to sit and watch the patterns shimmer in the sun
Iridescent and glowing
As my transfixion rebounds in waves to you

POET

Kind Weird Wild

Kind Weird Wild uses colorful and energized self-expression to forge new levels of creative liberation. By blending science and mysticism, he inspires to ignite that creative spirit that resides in all of us.

The Cycles

The cycles……….
The Patterns…………

Am I the one in control……..

Am I just a product of the autopilot my brain created during my early development……

Am I the one in control?

I heard that time is always happening all at once……
That the past, present, future is happening at the same time.

Then Consciousness is…..
…. Now

But Am I the one in control….

The weather is sunny, but a storm can happen at any moment.
Am I progressing,
or am I just becoming a better version of the person I was always meant to be.

Who were my parents before me?
Short. Shorts.
And a mustache that demands attention.
And A Yellow Van…
…that you know, is up to no good

But let's rewind.
It all started when a woman from Louisiana
Decided to pack up her station wagon and escape.

Armed with her two kids and pregnant belly
They drove out west…..

California has always been the place that people escape too.

The dream of a better tomorrow.

The souls that have always been wondering.
What is over that hill, that lake, that ocean…

Like most hero's,
This story starts in chaos.
No room to experience childhood…
Growing up had to happen fast.
That's where it all started.
A leader that had no choice but to lead….
A soul that new nothing of play,
where all choices had direct consequence.

That's the origin story that would shape everything to follow.
And..
At the same time,
Across the world….

Another story was unfolding.
A Matriarchal Lioness made a decision.
to leave her comforts and familiar life,
Hop on a boat, trek across the fucking
Atlantic Ocean….

And Land next the oxidized, copper goddess….
Here is where the tired, the poor, the huddled masses came
When they yearned to be free….

From here…..
Grace was born.
A soul that only comes around every thousand years or so…

A spirit that cannot be tamed.
In a world designed to tame, and shame, and blame…..
What happens when an unstoppable force
meets an immovable object,
A universe is created.

How do people meet?
Out of all the timelines, and all the paths
That intertwines and expands.

Now I see.
All the puzzles of our ancestors.
All the Struggles that were never processed.

Carry on.
They are alive….
As real as you and me…..

Now I see.
A puzzle unsolved
is a puzzle passed down.

Static Tornado

This static tornado makes me nauseous.
It’s like my brains lost at sea and the ships about to capsize.

It’s an art to live an effortless life.
To weather every storm and hope that it’s what nature intended.

To mix trust with the unclear and drink it down
with a smile. …….

You ever hear the one about the angels,
that we were accidentally left behind and forgotten,
who got taken in by some monsters,
until they forgot they were angels,
and believed they were monsters,
but then they remembered who they were,
So, they left the monsters,
But then the other angels wouldn’t take them back because they
were with the monsters too long,
So now they walk alone in an eternal spiral of light and dark,
that forever respawns to a world of absolute beauty and horror….

All while trying to pay the rent on time?
Ya, me neither.

Becoming a Flower

Our personal journey is just like a flowers'.

A flower lives many lives.

Each flower needs a different environment to thrive and flourish.

And when they do they rise,
They blossom
and peak.

They are gloriously Beautiful for that brief moment.

Then
they slowly
 wilt,
decay
and die.

But not a forever death.
They die until the environment is suitable to thrive once more.

We also need to die again and again to

grow strong.

So, Die
with
love and trust.

And Grow back again and again.

POET

Laura Ribitzky

Laura Ribitzky is pursuing an MFA at San Diego State University and holds a JD and MA. She is published in the San Diego Poetry Annual, 2021-2022 edition. Originally from Israel, she grew up in Boston and Atlanta, and lived and worked throughout the world. She currently resides in San Diego, CA.

Self-Portrait as Silence

What shape do you, my Silence take?
When did you start? (I think, before time.)
Where is your end?

Like a streaming water meeting
a rock that juts out
of the earth, you wash over me.

But I am not
a rock to be shaped
and smoothed,

and I dare not surrender
to the earth underfoot, its dirt
retreating from atop

the roots of trees, abandoning all,
exposing all in sublime
abomination, and I

of it,
neither above nor
below. The earth

is disloyal. Its silence
louder than your deafening
cacophony. It does not hear

Who Remembers the Cloud?

Consider the cloud: how
it drifts and floats
or coils and stretches and rages
in contortionist blows, then
simmers softly, exhaling
its final roars, until
it has given us
everything.

And in the ensuing quiet,
it lingers
for a moment
to pronounce:

I was here
I shouted my fury
I forced open the heavens
for you to see,
and now you know all.

But the sun's emerging rays
will soon pierce through
the cloud's fading remains,

and we will forget.

Consumed

I burn. My flesh smolders
into ashes. So I am,
so, I was.

Tingling to crackling to
a silence that remains.
The remains –

not the fury,
not the boredom,
not the in between,

the songs you sing,
the turn-aways and castaways,

the spark, the sparks, your
sparks for me,

the incremental fret
that grates and scrapes
and comes up for

one last breath.

POET

Le Reveland

Le Reveland (she/her) has been writing poetry and painting since a young age. She is an aspiring psychological social worker with a passion for helping people with mental illnesses and advocating against the stigma these illnesses still hold. Le is a mother to a six-year-old son and two fur babies, living with her forever partner who influences a lot of her poetry.

iron

i don't iron my clothes
i only have an iron for those little beads we made as kids

the shapes of hearts

and stars

under the pressure of the iron
the holes melt
blending them into one another

complete

if only the human heart mended that effortlessly

my iron has the button that draws the cord back in
like i wish i could grasp you back
like a slingshot

no thoughts
just pull

but if you press the button too much, it gets tangled
or comes out the other side
over pouring you could say

as i over pour
my cup

they say you can't pour from an empty one
but i know differently

i pour until the glass has shattered
and my hands are cut up

do the broken pieces suffice for giving?
to you?

more of myself

all of myself

the iron can't smooth out the tatters of my life
like it can the sheets that we wrap ourselves in
the sheets that have heard the most

if sheets could talk
they would ask the iron to repair the wrinkles

is there an incantation to fix our wrinkles?

are there enough bandages to cover the damage to my hands?

not only the ones from picking up the glass
but the evil that has talked through them
the bad dog that has controlled them

i'm a good dog

honey, part one

When you think about love, do you think about me?
The falling in love, the knowing your partner like you've known them your whole life
Who comes to mind

Your honey eyes can't heal the hurt
They were the same eyes I gazed into the moment we met
And the moment you said I do
And when I asked you to be mine forever

But if you had to choose
Would I be the one you'd want forever
Or would you go back in time

I wanted to write about your honey eyes in a better light
But the overcast of the past three months rolls in
My chest tightens
The disassociation sets in
And I don't know who you are anymore

Maybe I never knew who you were at all
A fictional character I formed in the depths of my mind
And I fell in love
As we both fell apart

Words can only get us so far
And the touch of my hands can only leave so many imprints
And my memory would be soon forgotten
Because you loved them first

I'll never forget the day you told me that you've had the same love as ours before
But you lost it

Second place
Placeholder
Same story every time
I’m grasping at you
But I’m losing my grip

honey, part two

I wrote the burnt portion of this before
with fading memories, and as much forgiveness as my body will allow
I would like to pick up where we left off
when there was nothing more than smiling faces
and warm embraces

not empty promises
and broken rings
broken things

broken me

broken you

we've done enough damage to call a truce

I miss admiring your honey eyes
that you presume are brown
when you look at me too deeply, green
my own little mood rings
portals to your perplexing soul

words cannot attest to the sparkle the sun illuminates unto them
both golden and earthy
grounding yet lifting
the softness to my harsh
the stability to my weaknesses

we found each other in a desolate forest
lost
lonely
at our ends…really

meeting a stranger, that was never really a stranger at all
hands barely touching
hearts excitedly pounding

I promise to never let the sparkle abandon you
abandon us
to the sunless depths we pulled each other from

the sun to my moon
I will adore you as I have in every lifetime

POET

Leslie Ferguson

Author of the award-winning memoir, When I Was Her Daughter, Leslie Ferguson is a Southern California native and former high school English teacher and college writing instructor who earned her MA in English Literature and MFA in Creative Writing from Chapman University. Leslie's writing centers on loss, love, hope, and the consequences of trauma, and she is passionate about helping other writers find the courage to tell their own stories. She works in the publishing industry and resides in San Diego, California, with one husband and two cats.

Last Sail

pyrite eyes
with stars inside
he is part of my past
plastered to memory
molded from a photograph
fitted inside a white long-sleeved tee
shy as he sits on the boat's starboard side
someone must've asked him a question
'cause his lips are parted, tongue about to move

we were fourteen then
and the future a
folded, unfinished map
the gray sky lowered
as we motored into the bay

Split/Unsplit

we are messy
without clear margins
spreading as far as
our trauma will reach/the wind takes the fire

each of us is
a being of opposite meanings
we are rough before ready/
smooth after rain
worn down by grief
in this paradox/story of this time
in which we live/die

each of us is cleaved/
split apart at the seam of self/

each of us is cleaved/
stuck together as someone else

we become unbecome/become unbecome
with the rise/fall of the sun
there is no self except in the passive
act of effortlessness

so I will try not to try
so I can see what I see
so others, but not the you that is you,
will know me as me

selected/presented naturally

am I fit for this experience/
do I survive in spite of/because of myself?

who/what ignites the flame
by which I am meant to burn/

burn bright/
burn high/
burn fast/burn deep/burn wide?

I Will

If you give me a peach I will not suck the seed
If you bury me in dirt I will not bloom
If you soften the earth I will not sink
If you run me a bath I will not drown
If you carry me to bed I will not cry
If you sing me a melody I will not sleep

I pride myself on resilience
If you misguide my gaze I will not squint

If we collide I will not blame you
Close my eyes anyway
I rarely know what I need

POET

Madison Victoria

"My name is Madison Victoria; I am a 22-year-old soup-lover, spoon-biter, and sky-watcher living in San Diego. As a reclusive writer on the spectrum, who developed an obsession with symbolism early on as means to find fiction in the literal, my creative projects center around bridging the gap between self and stranger through interpreting life like a dream with recurring symbols. Sometimes found at local open mics or giving handwritten notes to strangers, I am an aspiring typewriter poet with intent to publish my work, design a set of tarot cards, put together a website from scratch, and host events for uninhibited self-expression. My writing is heavily inspired by nature, numbers, sex, catharsis, anatomy, divinity, trauma, girlhood, the internet, technology, repetition, long lists, repetition, woo-woo, science, and synchronicity."

\- M.V.

I BRUSH MY TEETH LIKE A ROSARY AND SPIT OUT THE BLOOD

How fragile, these bloodied instruments of pearly luster.

Strong enough to chip porcelain and gnaw at flesh,
yet erode so quickly at the behest of tiny creatures with bellies full of sugar.

Is it safe to claim metaphor, that the words which passed
my own lips were what wore them down?

Rot begets rot, or were the words sickly sweet?
Perhaps neither.

It was the shame.

OH MOTHER

My mother, still so beautiful even as her roots reflect the soil,
as her gut swells with undigested instinct, and as her teeth grey and rot and fall

My lovely mother, ruled by Murphy's Law and the moon,
whose life moves something like an electron, like its quantum,
her intent and actions like position and momentum,
my Desperate Daughter's Concern another worry unknowingly written by Heisenberg

My mother, whose skin is littered with scars and suburban shrapnel,
the strength of her own blood is her kryptonite

Sleep walking mother, as distant as she is present,
keeping a promise only barely,
The Little Engine Who Could

"Pretty, pretty princess", forever 15,
arrested development,
the little rose on her ass

Another birthday card written on a napkin

Another goodie bag, gifts stolen from thieves

Another man, just another drug,
a love bomb, a screaming match, a failed romance,
a dead friend

Meth as medicine for how her angel body recoils
so far from heaven

Immortal and immune to human disease,
she can't trust home, she can't trust Earth, even as she's steeped in its dirt,
breathing in its fire and flora like a jaded dragon,
eyes red and weeping with the rain

Hoarding every space she claims, even if it's just the distance
between her shoulders, carrying home on her back

Her aura, pulsing mania

Turning her Sakura into Sanskrit
and her Sanskrit into slurring

Oh mother

Your little girl in another hotel, thinking vacation
not prostitution

Your little girl snuck through the casino, thinking arcade
not addiction

Oh mother

What do I say to this boy?
How should I do my hair?
Why do I think this way?
Has there always been rape?
Where are you now?
Where have you been?
Who were you then?
Do I cry like you?
Do I fight like you?
Do you know that man?
Why is he here?
Why are you talking to him and not me?
Mommy, why are you running from me?
Why am I running from me?

Mommy

I'm sorry
You're sorry

I love you

PENANCE

Walking by the church at night, I stop for the stained-glass glowing,
teaching,

to make art of faith against fear;

that we're married to ourselves;
that I have a lot of secrets;

that there's sex in every confession,
in every lie that makes us holy,

in the begging on my knees,
and in the anger I pray you see as a need,

my need,

to be weak, to shed my pain, to lose control,

to let you have it;

to let you read my face,
like a sermon,
flushed with hot-blooded secrets;

to let you spill your light into me
until it hurts,
until my confession comes
like a blister cut on sin;

to tongue the truth, like a wound,
until I can't taste what I've done

Cold is the night
that I can only wear shame

because I'd rather be sorry than alone,
because at least a punishment means you're there

Cold is the night
that I've snuck out the door

because love is being forgiven, not being good;
because the rise after a fall is that much greater, that it's head
change;

that the voice in my head telling me I'm not good enough is God,
not my family, not my species, not myself

Cold is the night
that the church is the only thing glowing, teaching,

that I have a lot of secrets
because I love to confess, I love to confess,

I love to confess

POET

MariaStella I. Cubias

MariaStella is another human writing about her experiences while courageously fighting feelings of being misunderstood or feeling undeserving. She has many titles, a depressed poet who dreams big and stays curious like a cat is just one.

Tony Z

My love,
I’ve shown my worst.
I'm afraid,
You have now seen all of me.

What beauty have I been blessed with?

Who knew and didn't bring notice to me?

The love that you provide,
I had not yet experienced it.

For someone to love all of me,

The pieces of insecurities,
You pluck off me,
Like no burden comes about.

My anxieties slowly fade,
Because the reassurance you provide me.

I’ve never let anyone inside,
But now I see, it was only meant
To be seen by a few,
One of them, being you.

Daughter

My bagged-up body lies below your glare,
Just beneath the chin.
Each pile of dirt placed on me,
Acts as the wall you put up between us.
I stick a straw through the black trash bag-
To sip up the tears you failed to show me-
When I said "I love you" for the last time, alive.
Your hate, I pray dissipates into the void.
I cursed you alive and protect you as the dead.
You wanted a mother, but I treated you as a friend.
I hope the anger I showered you with,
Does not translate into your worth.
I no longer want you to hurt.

The thoughts I leave alone

My eyes were closed when I saw myself in light
Holding your hand as your face stayed
Blurry,
I don't know why we were in
Such a hurry to smile and glide
Up in the sky

I began to cry as soon as I opened my eyes
It wasn't the place I wanted to be

The mountains and sky
It all upset me

The green grass and cars going fast

I am quite bitter

My mind is like the freeway that I'm on everyday
-Fast, on the go, and bad for the air quality

Everyone has stolen the best part of me

What can I say, only that you crushed the little spirit I had left
Ripped it away like my favorite toy, you hurt me like a mom

I wish it wasn't dangerous (personal)

But my mom's ashes take me to an intolerable place
Somewhere a vampire could lie for centuries
Still undiscovered

A place that's quiet, easy- comfortable for me.

I close my eyes again, I'm under the soil and head stone labeled
"Peace"

~Skipping and smiling, the music is loud, I kick up my feet, I'm in love~

My chest grows tight

With each blink
I'm reawakened by the wretched reality I've been placed to exist in

But it's all my perspective
To live or to die
At least I'm here again
A victim's trend

POET

Marjorie Pezzoli

Poet - Silk Painter - Storyteller. She is a shy ham who will pick up a mic. www.PezzoliArt.com

Transformation

Zombie flowers rise
	between my toes

eats away
	self-doubt

roots enter
	my bloodstream

pain of consumption
	is ignored

transformation
	worth it

bones become
	a trellis

tendrils
	fill my lungs

a chrysalis forms
	in my skull

milkweed pops
	through fingernails

seeds await
	the wind

clouds whisper
	soon

Haiku

Needles penetrate
Acupuncture for my Soul
Chakras awakened

Sunshine & Whiskey

Sunshine & whiskey

Sips create rosy cheeks
golden liquid burns with delight

Divine inner & outer glow

Still, I prefer to sip Gin & Tonic
with moonbeams braided into my hair

Lay on dewy grass
in body temperature midnight air

Skinny dip in the vernal pool
created by mermaid's tears

Eyes sealed shut
Starlight dances on the tips my lashes

Flickering patterns fill the sky
I become one with the atmosphere

Time to reach for the last sip
the ice has all melted

A slice of lemon greets me
my lips pucker for the awaited kiss

More than divine
make me another

POET

Michael Angelo Hernandez

Michael Angelo Hernandez is a musician, poet, and artist from Moreno Valley, California, currently residing in San Diego while attending university. Developing an interest in literature from a very young age and growing up a child of immigrants in a lower income community, themes of philosophy, politics, and spirituality are littered through his works which aim to paint his picture of the human experience.

Winter Vision Quest

for John Nathan Adams

I forgot who I was before my shower.
dried off, got dressed, and laid on the couch,
looking out toward the balcony.

Above me, the knots on the wooden roof,
scattered like stars,
twinkled in the bright light
beaming in from the sliding glass door.

Outside, snowflakes fell at a steady pace.
whistling winds whirled wisps of white
from up on the rooftops, down to the floor
and around the corner as if calling me over.

What lost things can be found
meandering the mountains of Mammoth?

Just off of Meadow Lane.
Up the pearl white street,
over the powdered bridge,
along the frozen creek
That still runs underneath,
I walked through the trees
and got caught in a cloud.

The morning ice melted at the touch of my fingertips,
crystals stuck to strands of hair before my eyes.
Revealing their translucence in the seconds they took
to slide down and dissolve from the warmth of my face.

That warmth had withered with the day,
my hands were freezing,
and the more I strode into the storm
the less I could see.

The roars of the cars and snowplows had faded into the ether.
the silence was enough to make you believe
you had lost your sense of hearing.
Were it not for the sound of your own narrow breathing
and the crunch that follows your every step.

There, in the forest.
past millions of pairs of eyes
that stare at you hidden from all directions.
A bench rests amongst dead trees.
When you brush off the snow
an inscription that reads:

A PATH TO AWARENESS
IS A PATH TO
GREATNESS. IT IS NOT
FOR MOST. IT IS FOR
THOSE WHO ARE THE
LIGHT IN DARKNESS.

IN MEMORY OF
JOHN NATHAN ADAMS
1971-2010

I let the letters swirl around in my head for a minute.
When I left, I thanked Mr. Adams (whoever he was) twice.
The first time for his seat to the weary wanderers of the forest,
and the second for his wise words.

With my numb hands I cleared his bench once more
before heading back into the blizzard haze.
As I noticed the weight of the ice on my shoulders
I began to wonder where I was headed.
I don't really know.
All I know is
the storm's picking up,
the sun's going down,
and I'm still a long way from where I want to be.

Mammoth, CA, Dec, 2021

I took a train to Merced

Surrounded by trees
submerged under spells of escape
captive still to my dark reflection
projected by the mirror surface
of a 2nd story bedroom window,
perched on a slanted rooftop
with red and gold stars all around
the inside and above my head.
As music plays from a speaker
a friend of mine sleeps
another draws eyes in my journal
and there's a white sign facing outside to where I am
in bold black letters
two words stare at me
'SEND HELP'
admitting me deep into a trance of wonder.
I've been awake for a while,
drove through the night
watching the ribbon highway unravel from behind a cracked windshield.
Slept a bit on the bus
stayed up the whole Amtrak ride writing nothing,
ditched my classes all the way on the other side of California,
called off work too
told them I was sick,
only half true.
I ran off,
needed a change of pace,
been needing a lot of those lately.
I spent the summer ripping up court letters
getting ripped off and robbed
by the banks and their bandits
while the cops filled up their pockets
making profit off us Others
Spent the summer losing everything I had,
everything I thought I was

as quick as the closing of my eyelids
was reminded what was mine
nothing

Lily of The Valley

For Rachel

Little lamb, pretty flower
sprouted from the tears of the first mother
how your bells hang their head in sadness
not knowing that it's you
who the sunflowers turn to

POET

Michael C. White

Michael is a writer of poetry, short stories, polemical letters, and essays. He is inspired by his work and travels as a young man from Cabo San Lucas to Queen Charlotte Sound and his extensive travels and work in Micronesia and the Indo-Pacific Region. He lives in Coronado, California with his wife Penelope. His daughter Catheran-Kealoha lives on Oahu and teaches at Mokapu School in Kaneohe.

Becoming a High Sierra Meadow

Begin with lightening and a thundering surprise!

Touching the earth's hard places with drops of rain, ice and snowflakes settling on high granite surfaces of the planet.

A blanket of ice and snow cover these high and hard places forming a white spread of purity and quiet solitude.

The melt starts with the lengthening arc of the sun and the heat of the season; drops, trickles, rivulets gather into a stream of energy.

Transformed from frozen purity into a gurgling, flashing crescendo of water, light and energy over a bed of granite. Giggling, laughing, cascading, sparkle ling, shooting off , colors of the rainbow with gravity inspired energy

Boundless unconscious of the inherent kinesis of reality. Singing down the course of granite and gravity. Unbounded unafraid, high in spirit, delighted in being the force of unstoppable optimism!

The thousand-foot escarpment threatens to become a fall of water leaping into oblivion
But that fate is shunted aside by granite reality. Swirling in confusion, circled around in a tempering of enthusiasm becoming a high lake with a rivulet draining down the side of the escarpment.

The settlement begins with the sediment brought down from high above. Memories of the granite, water skaters, and ouzels and the debris of gametes provide the first riches to provide growth.

On the sunny side the birth continues, beginning with growing plants filling the pure blue of the high lake with the green of living. Proceeding across the blue ever so slowly, when compared to the high energy birth.

Gradually the ebbing of the lake into a pond. sprouts life forms too
numerous to count. Insects, larva, frogs and fish. The spirit has been
quieted with the growing of the pond into the meadow.

The settlement with sediment becomes the reality of the growing
meadow. As the blue recedes into the meadow green the character
changes to become a home of larger things:
puddling ducks, marmots, deer, elk, wolves, and lions

The energy and unbounded spirit of gravity has become a place of
calm and complex drama of birth, sacrifice and rejuvenation
becoming with settlement, sediment and sentiment the meadow.

M. C. White August 22, 2014

Reputations

As to those stones that you cast upon the sea,

Some remain hidden forever in the abyss.

While others come back upon dry land tarnished and stained.

But when those same stones again are immersed in their element the sea,

And handed up to light of day they shine back at you

With a smooth lustrous patina and

Dazzling clarity

The Storm of the New Year

Oh yes, what a storm we saw together.

It was the day of the new year.

There we sat high on the cliffs.

Winds, storm tossed seas, perched there in a sheltered lee.

We were overlooking the tempest.

A lonely sea lion struggles to safety on the rocks below.

Do you remember?

It blew so hard my eyes were watering from the wind.

Or was it empathy and dreams of storms to come.

POET

Monarch the Poet

Monarch is a Black, queer, transgender poet who brings tragedy and triumph to life through his poetry. He's a slam champion and national touring poet, showcasing his art to audiences who need it most.

Worse Than Love

The worst thing anyone has ever said to me was
Let Me Go
Imagine
You wrap your arms around the person you love, taking in the serenity that is being in their embrace and their response is
Let me go
How do you describe the feeling of gripping the windowsill of their car door, while the gear shift is in reverse, begging them to stay just 5 more minutes and they say
You have to let me go
How?
How do I watch my heart leave me like that?
Do I pretend that none of this ever happened?
That you were a dream that came to me in the midst of a shroom trip?
What do you mean let you go?
How can those words force their way out of your mouth?
I was expecting I love you but instead I get
Let me go
This is killing me
I don't think you understand what you've done to me
Call me captain Cook
Because I'm dying here
Washed up on the shores of paradise
Only to have my heart ripped out of my chest
Call me Persephone
The weight of this grief has suppressed my appetite
Our love used to bring the spring flowers but now
I'd rather fight with Hades than suffer through the hell of losing you
Or call me teapot
Because the scream I let out when my emotions boil over is a signal that I can't handle the heat of this grief anymore
Call me Ikea
Because the next person that comes along will have to reassemble me but my directions are written in a language only you speak
Call me junk yard
Because I'm nothing but a shell of what I used to be
The pieces of me fell apart and rusted

You were the engine that kept me running and without you I'm nothing
But a broken-hearted poet
Call me
Just call me
Pick up your phone and tell me you love me
That you miss me
That you're thinking of me
Something
I'm begging
Please
Just let me breathe
It's easy to exhale
But I can't seem to find oxygen despite everyone around me still breathing with ease
How do I let go of the love of my life without letting go of my love for life?
This has destroyed me
I wish grief didn't exist
But grief cannot exist unless love was there first
So the worst thing I could have said to you is
I love you

Weight of the World

I want to kiss you
To feel the gentleness of your love
The passion that passes from your lips to mine is enough to jump start my heart
You are art
A masterpiece
And I know better than to touch murals painted by the gods
And if I leave my fingerprints on your canvas
I'll be removed from the premises
It's hard enough knowing I can't touch you, but I'd take the place of atlas and purposely fail if I wasn't allowed to even view you anymore

POET

Nick Henderson

Nick Henderson, Author, Writer, Poet, Editor studied undergraduate English at SDSU University; Earned his MFA in writing and fiction at CUNY Brooklyn College, where he also worked as an English Professor. He was a special education teacher in San Diego. Nick's Novellas, "Burning off Sin," and unpublished, "If We Were Sailors," include timeless Short Stories, Prose, and Poems, are inspired by people in his life whom he has loved and who have loved him; struggles encountered within the world which we live, past and present- their lives and his, the Human Spirit. "I have discovered that true bravery is found when you don't win much, but you try anyway. I am Nick Henderson."

I. In Jail

I want to scrape the jutting feathers
   from my back

I've lost my love for art

I want to take a step over the edge again

It's easier staring into an empty canvas

I can give it to all of you

Maybe you will see me then

Rather simple.

White shirt

Pair of Levi's

My eyes

Good tennis shoes
   holy socks

And a backpack
   with spoons
for peanut butter

When it's all gone
and everything has been set
   in its right place

I can look in the mirror

And I will see me

I will recognize myself

New snow without footsteps.

The trees have no leaves,
   or in the street

Yet they still hold their branches high

II.

My heart is a buoy
without anchor

floating on the surface
of my breath
rising and falling

high above forgetfulness

I want to push it down
press it in
in like a button

but it refuses to be submerged

It remains free floating
and
with the wind
and
the swell of the tides

vulnerable
far too honest with me
even cruel

I am awake all of the time now

underneath the sun

I've lost my shadow

She's left me here

to ponder the sky

Nick Henderson
December 22, 2017

III.

Sunshine Eyes

Freckles
with Flaming Lashes

Woman more than you or I

You cannot understand
You can't compare

It's a Life
that Breathes and Beats

under Waves
of Brutal Ocean

It's a Heart that Thunders
under Pressure

That can be Felt
and then Heard

Passive
but
Intentional Strength

It wants Protection

but doesn't need

more than

I Love you

Nick Henderson
August 9, 2015

POET

Robert Hammel

Robbie Hammel's life goal is to see a poet sell out the balboa theatre in San Diego. Not a charity show. Not a mixed show. Not an influencer/poet. A poet. Doing poetry.

A Chair

The important thing is faithfulness
in a chair, to trust where your rump is going.
It needs to be sturdy, but also gentle.
You want your spine to feel like a healthy flower stalk,
and the chair like a fine soil. Deep. Solid but
somehow very giving.

It ought not be too comfortable. A lot of people get
this wrong about their chairs. Comfort is
the sticky place where dreams hang on,
and chairs are not for sleeping.

The ideal chair is where comfort meets production,
or as I like to think of it:
where the ass can settle seriously.

I prefer wood without cushions of any kind,
but it has to be designed by some ridiculous Creator
who can make hard planks soft on your skeleton.
Maybe that's not possible. But
I've sat in ones that come close.

Conspiracies

In the hotel lobby
a sign by the front desk reads:
"there will be no waffles this morning"
and underneath this bad omen
the image of a half-man, half-waffle,
his shoulders roundly defeated,
hands in the air with fingers bent in anguish,
tired, surrendering. The waffle-man weeps.

There has been a waffle catastrophe,
some kind of massacre in the middle of the night
which the desk lady is hoping we don't ask about,
perhaps a flapjack uprising
or a pogrom on checkered skillets.
They are hiding it from us, this genocide,
and all we know is that today
"there will be no waffles."

In a Dark Apartment on the Poor Side of Town at 11:59pm

a man clears his browsing history
the pixels of his laptop stutter, the only light in the room like spilling
onto his face from a confessional window
"are you sure?" the machine asks him. He clicks. Clear history.

What deeds did the ancient man erase?
What did the young men of older generations, in their lonesome moments,
desire a button to scatter the tracks of their desires?

There's legend that Jean-Jacques Rousseau had a spanking fetish so desperate that
he used to position himself on street corners, ass exposed, hoping that unwitting ladies would
round the turn and strike him on his bottom in shock.

When another Frenchman, Robespierre's head rolled off the guillotine,
was there a man in the mob, maybe a child on his shoulders to get the view,
did they think they were erasing asses, or slaying gods?

-no, they wouldn't have thought a moment about the confessional.
Not for the ass or the divine. That older man and his child were hungry, no other shame.
That's what the German got wrong in the next generation, we did not slay God,
so many others did that for us, but there is a more terrible shame
in watching our father die and thinking: life will be easier without him,
good, we will move faster now, we will have a better chance hustling bread,
evading our own death.

But about that younger man, in his room, on the computer. He shuts it, until the next
high-definition wank, walks the dark hall to his refrigerator where it will light him in
frozen glory. It's all clear. It's all clear.

POET

Rose Curatolo

"I am a poet and a writer. Throughout my life, I've always enjoyed writing short narratives or short stories and Prose inspired by life events. Occasionally, I'd write poetry. Recently, I took up writing poetry in October 2019. My inspiration for writing poetry and prose came from my son, Nick. Nick was a writer, an author, a poet. and an editor. He had already written a Novella for his MFA Thesis. However recently, he had been writing and working on a second Novella, a compilation of short stories, prose and poetry. He recently passed August 2019, after which I found all of his writings. Nick and I shared a very close bond and an immeasurable love and many loved memories of joy, happiness and pain. When he passed, my grief and pain was raw. Inspired by my grief and pain, turned into that love and bond we had shared, my own poetry and prose writing arose."

-R.C.

I.

For Us

I Am Your Life

You Are My Life

Together we ARE Life

Two Hearts beating as One
  One Flame we Are

Two Spirits intertwined
  within Stardust and Planets
Evolving from the beginning

As the earth found Our sun
  it Blazed
    and found our footprints
      journeying
  toward predestined paths

~ Rose and Nick
Mama and Son

II.

Heart   Realm   Spirit

Hello my Dear Mama

There is..
a Realm where I am at
  It is the Same

I am There
with YOU
Now

it is the Same

it is pretty Simple

It is Different
but not
 That much different

I am Here
and that Is the Same

The Love is just as Strong
 and Felt
the Same

Our Bond
Is just as Strong
  and Beautiful

That Is the Same

Do you think you do Not see me ?
but
  you Do

And it is the Same

As Always

yet Different

I am There
Wherever You Are

That is the Same

I might be in the garage
-as usual this time of evening.

That is the Same

Or sitting right beside you on the sofa

That is the Same

I Am
Here as Always

That is the Same

I know you miss me
I miss you too

It is the Same

It is hard for me too

That is the Same

I want it to be like it was
because it is what we are used to

I want it to Be

The Same

as Usual

I want to Feel the Closeness too
but mostly for You

That Is the Same

I know you want to Feel my arms
Around you

Just know
my arms Are enclosing You
and
I am always right there With You
as Strong as ever

It is the Same

You can Hear me too

It is the Same
but

More

Our senses are more Heightened
Than
Before

So if you want to
Hear me,
just close your eyes
and

Listen

My Voice is the Same

If you want to
See me,
just Look

and

See me

See
My Face
My Eyes
My Smile

All
So Clearly

Just as Bright

It is All
the Same

I Am Here
With you

That is the Same

If you want to Feel
MY Heart Beating
put Your hand over Your Heart

It IS the Same
Heart

Heart Realm Spirit
Same

I Love you Mama,

and
That is the Same

Your Forever Loving Son,
~ Nicky

Nick Henderson and Rose Curatolo

Son and Mother
Poets, Writers, Authors
Cancer Warriors
Spirit Knights

III. "Girl from Brooklyn"

Girl from Brooklyn

Crying-crying sitting on a stoop

Sun on the Stone Lions
  Warming her hand

Old women in black dresses
Witches watching
  their cackles clog her tears

Black shadows- long silhouettes
Slithering sliming into whence they crawled

Girl from Brooklyn

Otherwise, soft Hazel
Hardened eyes pierced their evil
  casting a spell
Her pout sealed their fate
  cackling echoes

  You're crying again

Girl from Brooklyn

Fingers under eyelids
  and into nurturing mouth
Eyes rolling underneath darkness
  Silenced tongue

Girl from Brooklyn

Winding downward- spiraling stairs
Upon which she sits

She fears

No sight
No voice

It’s better that way

No tears

Girl from Brooklyn

Maple and Oak trees
Sun and shade
Roller Skates
Shoestring
Skate keys
Black tar street

Girl from Brooklyn

White rags then curls
Your Mama’s soft hands
Her kiss
Shiny locks springing
Bouncing
Bellisima!

Her Mama’s sweetness

Girl from Brooklyn

-Rose Curatolo
Poet
Writer

POET

Sara Froi

Sara grew up in a small mountain town and has been adventuring ever since. She writes poetry about religion, mental health, and being a millennial. She is a lover of reading, true crime podcasts, her dog, and her husband.

I Was Born a Fire

I was born a fire
And sometimes, I'm ashamed
I think to ask God why I explode whenever someone fans the flame
But I know these words would never escape my mind, my mouth, my pen had I been born any other element

So, give me something to burn
I feel that I'm turning to coals
I need something to ignite me so I can learn
From my mistakes, a degree in ashes is what I'll earn
Because all those bridges left behind me have crumbled

Sometimes I am a raging forest fire
One that Smokey warned you about
I consume everything that was once beautiful and full of life
Because someone made a small mistake that sparked against something dry and dying

Sometimes, I'm a bonfire, the life of the party
People grab their friends and toss their awful pasts into my burning soul
There's music and dancing and everybody laughs
As the night grows darker, I grow brighter, to illuminate the faces of friends becoming lovers
But these parties always end, and I am doused with a bucket of icy cold water from the nearby ocean, salty as my tears when I am left behind and forgotten

Sometimes I am a source of warmth
Heat in the fireplace, I make even the poorest of homes feel like a palace
I am docile, comfortable, controlled
Feed me kindling and I'll feed your late-night dreams and inspirations
I hear whispers of new parents finally relaxing after children are sleeping
And I know, as I die down, love is still alive

Sometimes, I’m a candle
So innocent and unnoticed
But when the power goes out I light up the whole room

I was born a fire
And I know that if I don’t control myself, I’ll burn you
You’ll be engulfed in my flames, and I won’t know what to do
But I promise I’ll keep you warm, I promise I’ll give you light
Please don’t put me out I want to keep you in my sight

I was born a fire
And sometimes, I’m ashamed

You Dress Like a Lesbian

"You dress like a lesbian," he says
And I'm trying to figure out if I should take it as a compliment
Or if I'm offended
Because as far as I know, I'm not a lesbian
But I also know that I like lesbians
Not because they're lesbians
Also, not in spite if it
Who someone likes, or wants, or loves shouldn't have anything to do with how they dress
Why is this even a component of contention?
Why are my emotions so unclear?
Why do I have emotions at all?

Oh. Right.
I was brought up to love everyone unequally
To judge everyone based on outdated beliefs
To steer clear of anything that made me look like I was sinning
And everything is a sin

I was brought up to wear t-shirts and long shorts
They gotta go past your fingertips
Even if your arms are long

I was brought up to wear shirts with a minimum sleeve length of three fingers
And a neckline that is just that – to your neck
Cleavage will cause a man to stumble and send you straight to hell

I was brought up to wear board shorts with swimsuits
Cover up what you can
Because your body can plant seeds of lust
And should be kept a secret
Even to yourself

I was raised to believe that legging are not pants
They were created by men to sexualize women
Because men are incapable of seeing women as anything but an object

And that is exactly what you are

I was raised to believe that becoming a wife is the ultimate goal
Save yourself for marriage
Feel guilty anyway

So maybe I never learned to attract the mal gaze
I never learned to attract any gaze
And I'm pretty sure lesbians know how to attract a gaze
They sometimes attract my gaze

Because **people** are **beautiful**
Bodies are **powerful**
Minds are **fascinating**
Who wouldn't be attracted to that?

What Is Love?

Love is nothing
Love is free falling off the highest building, a peaceful soaring, only to be hit with the shocking reality that you leapt too soon, only to die too young
Love is the painful screaming, ringing in your ears when you can't fall asleep at night
Love calls out to you whenever you don't want it to, only to be chased down by the fastest train, run down in the streets when all you wanted was to dance barefoot in the rain, with soft kisses as the wet, cold droplets slide down your tear-streaked face
Love is the birds singing every morning, a sad, sad song that can only mean the end is near
Love is black eyes, bruised alibis, and lies about where the scars came from, the ones that may never stop bleeding
Love is 1 Corinthians 13 shoved down your throat every day from the time you reached 12 years of age, but never remembering the true meaning behind God and his true reality that he truly loves you
Love is a word that has lost its meaning; overused and only said when we want something from each other
Love puts you on a pedestal so high, only to leave you behind, crying, on the ground, lying in a deep pit of despair

But then love picks you up.
Love carries you and holds you in its arms until you have cried your last tear
Love is the sun on your cold skin, warming the sidewalk where we once danced barefoot in the rain
Love is never asking why, never forgetting the past, and always remembering that the future is brighter and just up ahead
Love gives you a reason to live; an eminent light before you that can never fade
Love won't leave you behind, and when love finds you, love will meet you every day, waiting outside your lonely apartment, ringing your doorbell no less than eight times

Love is the beauty you see when you open your eyes to angelic streams of fragrant beams creeping through your curtains in the morning
Love lacks all judgment and simply exists
Love is everything.

POET

Softboi Mumble

Aka Richard Sue Hernandez, everyone’s secret boyfriend, a bilingual poncho-poet straddling the border between San Diego and Tecate. blurring the lines between love poems and erotica, occasionally dipping his toes into the existential void lover of pretty words, pretty women and pretty California burritos. do not resuscitate.

the ocean and the storm

she tells me what she wants
when she wants
and how
in the dark
in the moons absence
and the rooms stillness
her soft skin
my pressing lips
make quite music
like rain
gently kissing the water's surface
on the roaring ocean
crush your delicate frame
in my arms
gasping throat, you'd moan if you could
you beg for breath
but your pussy throbs with every gasp
makes it wet
enough to stop counting fingers
could you deny me?
whose is it?
the ocean waves crest and froth
the storm quietly rumbles

moonlit sweat

beads of sweat catch moonlight
making nightscapes
on your writhing back
my hands, eager cosmonauts
make their way
from hips
to shoulders
to cooing throat
only thing I will let escape my clutch
is your breathless moan
the taste on my lips
won't let me forget
the look in your eyes
the pain and the soothing
my hands and your soft flesh
blurred the lines between
where you and I spent most of the night
the ambient blue of 3:42
makes your nude body seem so cold
beads of sweat, turn to a thin glaze
your breast glow sinfully in the moon light
consume the night, like dry earth taking in a summer rain
I watch you breathe…. quietly
dream of a sin so lovely
maybe behind closed eyes I'm worth the trouble
a man best loved in the dark
where sin and holy scripture share pages

sugar cane

I cling to pouting pussy lips
sipping sweet and salty nectars
till tightening thighs
suffocate me so lovingly
my very breathe
sucked from my heaving chest
squirming and cumming
slick, slippery tongue
feels around our mouths
finding froth, flavors and syrupy love
a strained moan
you want it
but you can’t handle any more
my grip
pressed red into your sweaty thighs
I put all of it in my mouth
suck it like sugar cane
drinking you all up

POET

Stephanie Roche

ESTEPHANI. Stephanie Roche is a native to San Diegan. She write's expressing LGBTQ+ life, grief, mental health, and life coaching. She does spoken word around California in local open mic communities. Her poetry has been featured in the anthology Fuck Isolation: A Tribute to the COVID-19 Experience (2020).

Odometer

I don’t drink.
I don’t smoke.
Now when I do it makes me choke.
All I do is lay down.
Pray and grind through all aspects of my day.
I don’t have time for fake and
unaware people that really need to heal.
The ones that did me wrong.
I don’t get upset for long.
I’ll still be kind from a distance reminiscing on the joy that I
continue to have.
Keep counting the miles.
Keep pushing.
Keep it one hundred.
Look at yourself in the rearview mirror.
Feel all the frequency the journey has set before you.
Some of you may no longer ride in my car.
We left each other in our individual chapters.
I wish you the best.
You know that was the universe.
Letting you know this is goodbye for now.
I am over here high on life and the righteous blessings I’ve obtained
and will gain down these endless roads.

- *ESTEPHANI (Stephanie Roche)*

POET

Sunny Rey

Sunny Rey, Founder and CEO of Poets Underground. Mother of 5, forever partnered with her beloved Anthony Azzarito. Advocate, Believer, Poet.

The Re-Opening: Ode to Poets Underground II

And what might it take
to step out of a man's headspace grave;
convince thyself that the clock has struck midnight
that the turn over into a new dawn has in truth begun.

Where once it was left without trembles ticking
The hours frozen in tears that found will to continue weeping,
Lived a candle high on a mantle of hope refusing to be snuffed out
by the brewed fog of confusion and fear.

For a human heart was made for this
Built with foresight knowledge of all it would need to muscle strong
to resist

And resist we did.

We surely won
as feet marched down in
the underworld for spoken word fun.

We made it to the reopening
We made it back to our stage

Tattered clothing turned gold
Mic unplugged while wild wind blows out our mouth from our brave
lung caves

Silenced never is a poets will and wit and worth
For it is he and her whom have
sat in the background writing out the destiny
of which this reopening would be set in stone tablets for

Never budging on morals in sandy lines
No, unless all could be included the reopening time waited on
standby

But oh here finally in celebration
The merriment bell no longer hesitant

crowd burst through painted doors
bones rattle a holy resurrection of the collective soul.

Seat one packed next to seat two
Germ shared with germ old and germ new
Inhale and exhale.
The glory of this night grows and glows over the nearby sky rise,
to a moon that never fails us and a God that never leaves.

Ode to Birth Day

Someone on Instagram sent me something from Tic Tok
That said that someone else told them
The great solar flash is coming

As I prepared to search this so called “event of my lifetime” up
I noted that safari still had “23andme” logged in
And I glanced at my digital family tree

There’s no one like me
I think to myself
A chart filled out with lopsided branches of my mother’s side

I was born into homelessness and into the week of mystery and imagination
My dad, to this day, is only known by the name on my original birth certificate before it became expunged at my adoption

I know nothing about him, but the tales some blood relatives would recite of him being a truck drivers’ son, and my mom hitchhiking a ride some random night

I’m grateful I was born into a San Diego hospital
I’m grateful my uncle talked sense into my mother to leave me there
I’m grateful I had so many laughs with my friends growing up over crushes, over mischief, over attempts at home kit hair dye and haircuts and high heels for the first time
I’m also grateful for the painful times, addiction, family secrets I took cuts to the side to unwind, running away, losing my mind, finding myself romantically lost over and over again just to be found inside soft strangers’ beds and one liners and bars that stunk all the time

I’m grateful for my children
And the times good and bad I have with them
For my partner that God finally brought into my life

I'm grateful for Poets and poetry and working with the homeless population as a way of meeting my own way out of poverty lines and filling my soul's intention on a nine to five.

I'm grateful for 40
I'm aware of the knockouts that tried to get me
But I rose to the top every time

Not everyone gets this
This beautiful mess of a quest
I understand my journey unfolding the closer I get

As I reach over and take a deep breath
counting down with a small group of family and friends
I blow out magnificent glows over icing,
for another year full of blessing.
Poets Underground beats a pound in my chest with the birthday cheer dying down for the night,
until next year when we all write a novel again together,
now that feels like the luckiest birth right.

POET

Sydney Fogel

Sydney is a writer living in San Francisco. She attended Boston University and credits Room 222 on Bay State Road for igniting her poetic spirit.

Redwood Tree

My roots, an anchor,
they keep my wisdom steady.
I dare not sway:

I've watched for more than a lifetime,
and each lifetime after that
But I remain silent in my judgments.

My branches, paintbrushes,
drawing lines through the clouds,
cutting light like glass,
a mosaic at your feet.

My leaves
dripping with color,
the pigment oozing from every needle
but the supply does not drain.

One drop on your shoulder
engulfs you with fear,
and you're drowning
against my strength

Like Cancer

You think you do but you
don't really understand

the way it spreads:
when you hide something

it never stays hidden for long,
the remnants of the body always float
to the top of the lake.

You're a wreck –
communion from a hospital bed,
the meaninglessness of it all

and how suddenly everything has a meaning
that you just can't seem to comprehend.

You plant your fears somewhere else,
displace them so they can grow like

cancer, buried and discreet,
and never have a name.

Everything you've been blocking
out has been laying weight on me,

the body pinned to the bottom,
unfurling with disease.

Santa Barbara

Sand invades the plastic pail,
exfoliating the scored sides
and crowding every curved edge.
We scrape the surface clean, neat,
my palm pressing against the damp mass
so condensed, it barely leaves a mark:
the millions constitute one.

This stretch of land is my endless stage.
I dance, twisting my body
to fit the angles, I believe construct the perfect pose.
The spotlight never moves from above:
polka dots on my bathing suit
reflecting the light like numerous suns.

We build a palace —
following my father's recipe
like I followed the erratic placement
of his feet across the sand.
His hands, like tools,
carve the moat that I run to fill,
and with every second, the sand
sucks more water deep into its gut.

POET

Taryn Tyler

Taryn Tyler couldn't read until she was eight but wrote her first manuscript when she was thirteen. Literature is her favorite way to interact with the world. She currently lives in San Diego where she drinks way too many mochas and tries to walk her rapscallion rescue dog, Bronte.

Once Upon a Blue Moon

An orb dangles over a madman's head,
Scattering shards of joy into the night,
Like a chiseled soul or an ancient rune.

You speed past, eager for a safe, warm bed,
Too weary for shattered dreams of such height
Once upon a blue moon

You do not see my fire's reflection.
You do not dare feel the burnings of yours.
You battle your desires, blind and immune

To the molten gurgle of emotion,
Rotting behind a legion of doors
Once upon a blue moon

I will not hear your doom filled lament
Nor heed your defeat infested advice.
I hear Truth in the giggle of a lune.

Though it is twisted and weary and bent,
My soul still simmers against chills of ice
Once upon a blue moon

A romantic's dirge and a rebel's rant
Are wound together in the sky's embrace,
In the timeless glow of a reacher's tune.

The impossible becomes midnight's chant
Sung in the winking of the moon man's face
Once upon a blue moon

Blank Page

A blank page stares at me like a hungry cat.
Fear clogged passages clamor for words,
Fogged with the dusty noise of my past.

Old dreams hum to me in forgotten lullabies
The relentless dance of thoughts churn in my head,
Hidden from reality by repetition.

If I could bleed ink, I would let it drip.
I would smear it across the page
Until the chatter was drowned.

If my lips were silent,
If my mind were still,
Could I form a word?

Elijah

(for Elijah McCain)

Violin strings cut through my heart,
Dripping deep red beads of music
Onto the ground in splattered pools
Of hope, once clenched in a fist of rage.

Neither fire nor storm nor plague
Can cleanse the earth where innocence
Was beaten and strung like a slab
Of your shriveled, vacant soul.

Phantom notes play like ghosts in our minds;
A loop of cruelty stuck on repeat
As you try to choke out the harmony
With your gas and our tears,

But you cannot stop music from breathing.

It will leak through the roar of your gunshots.
It will sink through the gasps in our screams.
Memory will screech with the blood song
You wrote when you slaughtered his dreams.

POET

Trevor Wing

Trevor Wing is a writer from San Diego, CA. His work tends to cover mental health issues, the deadly effects of social media, and the concept of apathy. He wants to believe, but nihilism seems a lot easier at this point in his life.

Studio

The Public Enemy record is the only thing audible in the kitchen/living room/bedroom/bathroom area of the house. This is a studio apartment. This is San Diego and all anyone can afford is a studio. The whole city is studio apartments. 3 people per studio. $2,500 for a studio. Everyone who lives in the studio works at a restaurant or bar and takes two community college courses a semester. 6 units. "Yeah, I worked a double last night" is the most commonly used phrase in the city. It echoes through the alleyways. Every time it's said, another cigarette is smoked. All waiters – sorry – *servers*, all *servers* smoke cigarettes on their 10's and their lunches. The cute type of smoking though. La Jolla smoking. Not the COPD, lung cancer, ruin your life type of smoking. We're talking like the "127 likes on Instagram" type of smoking. The "I went away to Humboldt State and came back after 3 semesters" type of smoking. Everyone drinks in their studios. Only craft beer. Only microbrew. San Diego has the best beer in the world. It's all small batch. Everything is an IPA or a stout. If you drink a lager, you obviously haven't been working enough doubles because money is tight. Don't forget to use coasters in the studio. We want our security deposit back and this isn't our furniture. We signed a 72 and three-quarter month lease for our studio. The market is tough in San Diego. Need to sign longer leases to get a better deal on our studio. There's no rent control for our studios. Lots of homeless people in San Diego. There's a homeless man who lives outside of my studio. Must of not worked enough doubles. He is drinking a craft beer though. Small batch. Microbrew. Everyone has a dog in their studio. French Bulldog or Pitbull. 400 sq.ft. 3 people, 2 dogs. $100 deposit and $50 monthly fee for each dog in our studio. Our studio is on the 3rd floor, so the balcony is covered in dog shit. It starts to pile up outside our studio. During winter it's fine, but the hot sun of summer increases the horrible smell outside our studio. Why did we get dogs when we work so many doubles? We're too busy to even be at our studio. We'd move out of our studio if we could. There's no 1 bedroom in San Diego. It's either studios or $5 million beach houses. I'm texting our studio group chat. We need more roommates if we're going to get a house. 15 roommates altogether to be able to move out of our studio. I've always wanted to raise a family. Definitely not in our studio though.

There are leftovers everywhere and dirty laundry is piled to the ceiling. It smells like cigarettes in our studio. Cigarettes inside, dog shit outside. I walk downstairs to get some fresh air. The 5 freeway runs right over our studio. The cars scream at me every time I leave our studio. I found a girlfriend and she now lives in our studio. We got engaged in our studio. We got married in our studio. We had kids in our studio. I didn't die in the studio though. I died in the restaurant. I was working a double.

Lab Rats

Others have spent a season in Hell, but I've been living in it for years.

I dwell within the depths,
I mingle with the madmen,
I play the bongos in the drum circle of the damned.

Orderlies let us put on tattered clothes and shed our hospital sheets. Sheets which resemble togas, but we were never people of high-standing in some theater of democracy – we are loonies, the town crazies, the pariahs with no messiah.

We pace around hospital rooms, walking from wall-to-wall waiting for someone to stop us.
No stimuli.
Nurses feed us chalk in a cup. We choke it down so we can maybe one day chat with the outside world again. At least that's what everyone wants from us.

But we are the bastard children of bureaucracy, and we would renounce our family name if we had one.

We are kept in an antipsychotic amniotic sac – alive but subdued.

We dance in front of royalty reluctantly. We entertain as court jesters but speak in jargon after our shift is over. We are subjects of no one. We are not loyal to any liege or lawmaker.

We are Prozac prostitutes pimped out by PhD's, but we still prevail.
With side effects as our sidekicks, we still prevail.
With stigma as our soulmates, we still prevail.

The last generation of us were lobotomized and electro-shocked; cut up and microwaved.
No community solutions so we are treated as expendable. Discarded and left to rot.

We're overpoliced and underfunded.

We tell people we are drowning, and they tell us to grow gills
They impregnate us with sleeping pills and
the side effects of these sedatives make us quite ill with
nausea, dizziness, fever, chills and
blood-red pharmaceutical companies sniff green dollar bills and
we tell them that we're finished, that we've had our fill but
they say they're going to keep us for observation because
we're a danger to ourselves and others still.

Mental anguish. Physical prison. This is the psych ward.

Patients and people from the outside world – who needs protection from who?

Casino

Big room.
Sprawling, in fact.
People slowly closing in on bright lights like wingless moths.
It is still 1986 in here.
Reagan is trickling slow and molasses-like down the walls of this place.
Smoke detectors on the ceiling. They can't work, right? Of course not.
Smoke wisps and congregates above, sliding along the high, smooth ceilings.
Ash on the floor. Looks like fucking Chernobyl.
The cold war continues on the craps table.
A man who hates Russia is playing roulette.
A vest and bowtie are throwing spades down on the table and wearing hearts on their sleeves.
Bloody Hell, Mary - another Bloody Mary, already? It's 6am.
Fuck off, buddy, she hasn't even gone to sleep yet.
All you can eat. Binge at the buffet and purge at your place later.
Later is relative.
There are no clocks here.
No ticking hands to give one incentive to leave.
This is a one-stop shop.
You'll never need sunblock again.
Fuck you, Coppertone, I'm in the zone.
This isn't luck, this is strategy.
I am a strategist. Move over Sun Tzu.
This is numbers.
This is mathematics.
I am a mathematician.
I am a genius.
That is why my partner left me.
I got home and no one was there.
Checked everywhere.
Looked at the high, smooth ceilings.
Walked into the empty living area of the house.
Big room.
Sprawling, in fact.

2023

...and it is so.

Meet Sunny and Anthony, the Founder/CEO and COO of Poets Underground Press LLC. Their passions drive from their love for God, their 5 children, their inclusive community and the arts. The couple runs writing events, open mics, writing & preforming workshops, retreats, partners with schools and community service events; in great effort to foster healthy individuals and communities. Known for their partnership publishing programs, they welcome all aspiring writers to apply.
poetsundergroundpress.com

We are Poets Underground.

Made in United States
North Haven, CT
03 January 2023

30577249R00134